MW01697569

Fatal Kiss

Suzanne Barr

The Write Stuff, Inc.

Fatal Kiss

Published by The Write Stuff, Inc.

Cover Design by Total Concept

ISBN 0-9766079-0-5

LCCN 2005901187

First Printing: March 2005

Acknowledgments

I truly appreciate those that helped provide information for this book. First and foremost, my deep gratitude goes to Susan Manning. Without her, I would not have known of this tragic story. Throughout the writing of this book, Susan was my right hand. Not only is she a great "assistant," she is my dearest friend. Susan and Ed, you both are priceless. The citizens of Kinston welcomed me into their fold with open arms. Those that took the time from their busy lives, I thank you. Stuart Johnson, Rick Vernon, Reece Gardner, Carolyn King, Debra Schreckengost, Carolyn and Paul Dunne for the material they so graciously provided, North Carolina Chief Medical Examiner Dr. John Butts, Matthew Martin and Woodrow "Woody" Taylor. A special thanks to Teresa White-Murray, her husband Johnnie, Steven White, Dan White, Leslie and Geneva White for allowing me to dredge up many unhappy memories. I could not have written this book without the support of my family. My husband Jay, who has supported me and encouraged me from the beginning. Amy, Jason, Lauren and Michael for allowing me time to work. My sister Marlene for her much-needed help, my Mom and Dad for listening to me moan and groan.
Any mistakes in the details of this story are mine.

Suzanne Barr
February 2005

For Little Bill

Fatal Kiss

There are few women so perfect that their husbands do not regret having married them at least once a day.

LA BRUYERE, *LesCaracteres*

PART ONE

Prologue

I shall see his toys and his empty chair,
And the horse he used to ride
And they will speak with a silent speech
Of the little boy that died.

June 21, 1973
Lenoir Memorial Hospital, 3:00 P.M.

Joshua Davenport Robinson's words might have been uppermost on Peggy Chrisco's mind that warm afternoon when four-year-old Billy White was rushed through the double doors of Lenoir Memorial Hospital's emergency room, or she may have thought this warm afternoon was just another ordinary day in the emergency room.

Until the doors flew open and she saw the hysterical woman and what appeared to be a sick child. Her instincts kicked in and she began to practice what she was trained to do.

Peggy had spent her entire life in Kinston, North Carolina. She'd been working as a licensed practical nurse for over a year now in Kinston's ER and was getting accustomed to seeing children as patients, especially during the summer. Most of them were stitched up, bandaged, maybe a prescription was needed, and then they were sent on their way.

However, nothing could have prepared her for the lifeless body of the beautiful blonde child that lay on the stretcher that June afternoon. It would have so much impact on her that it would change her life and many of her habits forever.

Between three and four years of age, he wore a pair of shorts and a small T-shirt. Upon close examination, Peggy spotted a small loose-fitting bandage on the child's lower right leg. She touched him. Like marble, his skin was cool to the touch. She tried to resuscitate the child but was unable to get a response. She so hoped there was something they could do for the little guy, but at this point, she knew it was hopeless.

In all the commotion during the child's arrival, Peggy had heard that he'd swallowed some plastic. She took a tongue blade and peered down the child's throat.

"There's nothing there," she said to ER nurse and good friend Susan Manning.

Susan stepped to the head of the table where the lifeless body of the child lay. She peered down his throat and also saw nothing blocking his airway. She held the child's neck gently in her hands and pushed his head back hoping that this would enable Peggy to see the obstruction.

"I can't see a thing." Peggy's words were laced with concern.

Susan peered down the child's throat. "I don't see anything, either."

"I'll call the doctor." Peggy went to the telephone. She dialed the number for the physician on call. It was Dr. Frank Sabiston.

Several minutes passed before Peggy and Susan saw Dr. Sabiston. His office was just across the street and to Susan it seemed as though the doctor had taken an exceptionally long time getting to the ER. However, in all the commotion with the nurses coming and going in and out of room trying to comfort the family, surely, Susan thought only a few minutes had passed.

When Dr. Sabiston arrived he went to the table that held the unmoving body of the young child and proceeded to examine him.

"What happened?"

"The mother said he choked on a piece of plastic, but we couldn't find anything."

"Let's have a look." Dr. Sabiston said. Peggy gave Dr. Sabiston a laryngoscope so that he could view what, if anything, was blocking the child's airway.

"There is something there. If I can just. . . ." He took a Kelly Clamp and inserted the instrument down Little Bill's throat. At the end of the long clamp were steel-like teeth that would grasp whatever they clamped onto. Once closed, the Kelly Clamp stays in position until released.

Susan remained at the head of the examining table where the child's lifeless body lay and thought of her own son, Allen, who was about the same age as her patient. Tears clouded her vision as she imagined her son in place of the young boy. Thinking of the grief that the family was sure to suffer overwhelmed her. She couldn't wait to go home to reassure herself that her own child was safe from harm.

Anita McGirt asked him to remove the plastic."I see the tip of something." Dr. Sabiston said. With the Kelly Clamp he removed a clear looking object, which appeared to be a large piece of plastic that had been wadded up into a ball.

Dr. Sabiston dropped the plastic into Susan's hand then left the examining room. She plunked the vicious looking piece of plastic into the sink and turned back to the doctor. The thoughts skittering through her mind were wicked. She couldn't go there. She wouldn't go there. Not now with the family needing her attention.

Susan didn't recall in her nurse's training where they

taught you what to do in situations like this. Fortunately for her, it was the father who broke the silence.

"He's always been accident-prone." Billy White said, his voice laden with unshed tears. "He's still wearing the bandage from his last accident."

Both nurses and Dr. Sabiston observed the bandage on the child's leg. Billy told them that had just happened a few days ago.

There was nothing left to say. The Whites had just lost their youngest son to a tragic accident. They told the nurses the name of the funeral home they would use and left the room.

Susan completed the required medical forms then went to the sink to look at the plastic the doctor had removed. She was beside herself. There were no signs of tear marks, no signs where someone might have tried to tug or pull at the plastic in order to remove it from the boy's throat. There was no smell of vomit, something that should have occurred if the child had gagged on the plastic. There were no scratch marks from a fingernail. Nothing at all indicated the child had tried to expel the object by natural physical mechanisms.

Often Susan would wonder how such a small child could swallow such a large object. *Accidentally,* it would state on the death certificate.

* * *

CHAPTER ONE

The endearing elegance of female friendship.

When Billy White met Sylvia Ipock, they were both living in Kinston, North Carolina on Roseanne Drive. Billy, along with his four children, Teresa, Danny, Steven, Little Bill and ailing wife Anita, lived at one end of the street, while Sylvia Ipock with her three sons, Jeff, Tony and Todd resided at the opposite end of Roseanne Drive.

Touted as the "All America City," Kinston was the sort of place where one could feel safe with their children out on the streets, even after dark. Brick homes with well-tended lawns and tidy flowerbeds, Roseanne Drive was an above average neighborhood, a place where one didn't have to lock their doors at night. So trusting were its citizens, it wasn't unusual to pass a roadside fruit market left unattended. In place of a cashier one might find what Kinstonian's refer to as an "honor box." An individual decided what was a fair amount for the products and left it inside the box. In the summertime watermelons were sold throughout the county in this way.

Surrounded by small farming communities with names like Deep Run, Moss Hill, Pink Hill and Snow Hill, Kinston is the twenty-second largest city in North Carolina. Lenoir County boasts three incorporated municipalities, Pink Hill and La Grange with Kinston serving as Lenoir County's seat. It is the center for the county's industrial, commercial, and financial trade.

In 1759, the General Assembly of North Carolina passed an act to establish three tobacco inspection warehouses in what was then called Dobbs County. It was at the sight of one of these warehouses, located along the banks of the Neuse River that "Kingston" was originally established. The community was named for King George III of England. Years later, Kingston was renamed Kinston.

Billy C. White had spent his entire life in the Kinston area. He saw no reason to relocate, move to the big city. Kinston was the ideal city in which to raise his family.

Billy was about to start his climb up the ladder of success. However, with four children, Teresa, Danny, Steven and Little Bill, a mentally ill wife who was in and out of the hospital on a regular basis, not to mention trying to establish himself in the insurance world, was more than any man should have to handle alone.

* * *

Sylvia Ipock would observe her neighbor's comings and goings. Tall, handsome, and rumored to be virtually single, she made it her personal mission to be indispensable to the White family.

Widowed in 1967 and left with three boys, Jeff, Todd and Tony to raise when her second husband Leslie Ipock shot himself in the head, Sylvia the ever-efficient neighbor, was a dream come true for the struggling White family. Billy thought his neighbor attractive and longed for more than friendship with the bubbly woman, yet he kept these thoughts to himself. He was still married, after all.

However, life inside the White household was about to change. After a disastrous fight with her daughter Teresa, Anita was diagnosed with schizophrenia and committed to Dorothea Dix, a mental hospital about eighty miles away in Raleigh.

Never knowing what to expect while Anita was home, or what kind of mood she would be in when he came home had been stressful enough. Now with Anita hospitalized, and he was sure it would be permanent this time, Billy now had to round up his children, make dinner, spend quality time with them and let them know they were loved. After he saw to Little Bill, who was barely over a year old at the time, he spent the remainder of his evenings conducting business at home.

Finding a friend and confidante in his neighbor was an added bonus. Billy White was very impressed with Sylvia and her domestic skills. Alone with three young boys and a home to care for, Billy never saw any evidence of neglect. Sylvia herself always dressed respectably and the boys' clothes were always clean and well-ironed. Billy could only wish for such orderliness in his disorderly life.

With Anita temporarily out of the picture, it was at this vulnerable point in Billy White's life that Sylvia chose to make her move. Equipped with hot meals and a woman's touch, the White family welcomed Sylvia's assistance.

After much deliberation Billy White divorced Anita, who remained institutionalized. There was no doubt in Billy's mind that he was doing the right thing. Anita would never be able to function normally. He owed it not only to his children, but also to himself to try and make a decent home life for them

After a hasty divorce from Anita, which she strongly objected to, on December 3, 1971 Billy and Sylvia were married. Though not a marriage of passion, it was certainly one of needed companionship and Sylvia a much-needed mother for his four children. Billy and Sylvia merged their two families without much hoopla.

With seven children between them, minus Teresa who was now living on her own, the first item on the agenda of the newlyweds was to find a bigger house.

North of Roseanne Drive, Billy and Sylvia found the perfect home in the private community of Westhaven. For a family the size of Billy's and Sylvia's, Westhaven with its many amenities was ideal. There the children could play freely. On hot summer days and warm evenings Westhaven's private swimming pool would almost always be occupied by the White-Ipock children.

Billy had made the right decision. Life was good. His marriage to Sylvia couldn't be better. The children were adjusting well to their new life . . . or so it appeared.

* * *

Billy White's older brother, Leslie and wife Bonnie were frequent visitors at the home of the newlyweds. Even though the couple had six children living at home, Bonnie was constantly amazed by the orderliness in the Ipock-White household. She wondered how Sylvia managed. At that time there were no Martha Stewarts or Hints from Heloise. You either had it or you didn't. Sylvia was as organized and efficient as a Drill Sergeant. She did spring cleaning almost on a daily basis. There were no cobwebs or dust moats in her home. On certain days of the week one could find her giving orders to the older children on how to clean beneath their beds. Stripping sheets, removing the mattress and box springs, and taking the bed frame apart was all part of her weekly cleaning ritual. She made sure the older children became quite accomplished at these tasks.

Still, there was the matter of Little Bill. When she married Billy, her children were pretty self-sufficient. They went to school, did their homework, cleaned their rooms, then spent the rest of their free time doing whatever young boys of that age did. Sylvia always assumed that they were at the pool or out riding their bikes in the neighborhood. She didn't really care as long as they were out from under her feet. However, there were rules that the White children knew they must live by, unless they were willing to suffer the consequences. One of those rules was to never lie to their stepmother. She would make it her mission to find them out if she thought they weren't telling her the entire truth, then there would really be hell to pay. More often than not, the children behaved and did as they were told.

Little Bill continued to present a problem for Sylvia. At two he was barely old enough to understand her commands, let alone follow them. A two-year-old certainly could not be expected to go a day without some sort of mishap. It was these "mishaps" that Sylvia could not deal with.

* * *

CHAPTER TWO

Oh, call my brother back to me!
I cannot play alone:
The summer comes with flower and bee –
Where is my brother gone?

June 21, 1973

Nothing seemed out of the ordinary that Thursday afternoon for ten-year-old Steven White. Just another summer day. He and a few buddies swam and roughhoused in Westhaven's pool. Steven, along with his older brother Danny and two step brothers, Tony and Todd, were all having a good time that warm summer afternoon.

Steven thought just about anything had to be better than hanging around the house. When his stepmother was nearby, he had to be very careful because anything he said or did might be taken the wrong way. Sylvia's wrath was something the White boys could do without.

Steven wondered why his father put up with her. It wasn't like she was pretty or anything. The only thing Steven thought she was good at was cleaning house. She reminded him of the wicked stepmother portrayed in Cinderella. Secretly, though, he thought she was much worse. Like the time when he'd gotten into a fight with Todd. She'd been enraged, her cold blue eyes flashing like shards of broken glass. "If you ever touch one of my boys again, I'll strip you down to your bare ass, and then I'll tie you to a tree. I'll beat you like you've never been beat before!" She'd smirked then added, "And I'll make sure all your friends are here to watch."

What would her church friends think of her if they heard her say all that mean stuff? What would they think if they heard her calling the Preacher a "goddamned idiot?" No doubt she'd continue to deceive her friends and his dad as she normally did and make him out to be the liar.

As young as he was, Steven knew something wasn't quite right with his stepmother. It was like she was two different people. At home she was wicked and hateful to him and his two brothers. But in public, she was so sweet and kind, Steven often wondered if it was the same woman. She certainly didn't behave like his friends' moms.

For instance, when she brought groceries home and put them away inside the cupboard. They had a "good" side of the cupboard where all the name brand foods such as Pop Tarts and Skippy peanut butter were kept. Then there was "the other" side. The side that held all the generic brands. The White boys were allowed to eat from the other side of the cabinet only. The name brands were reserved exclusively for Tony, Todd and Jeff.

Steven would tell his dad about Sylvia's behavior and hope for some interference on his, Danny's, and Little Bill's behalf. But Billy White was a peaceful man and would do anything to please his wife, even if it meant bribing the boys. He would simply offer them a few dollars to buy whatever they were whining about and apologize to them once again for their stepmother's behavior. It wasn't that Billy White didn't love his children. He did with a passion. Buying them off was just a lot easier than dealing with Sylvia's ranting and raving.

It was times such as these that Steven wished his real mom wasn't sick. He'd bet anything that she wouldn't treat him the way Sylvia did. He wasn't really sure what had happened to his mother, but according to Sylvia it was his fault that she was in the hospital. "After your mother gave birth to you, she tried to kill herself, and then tried again after having Little Bill." Steven felt sorry for Little Bill. He'd never had a real mom because she'd been sick for so long. Poor Little Bill called all women "mama."

At ten Steven was too young to understand the meaning of postpartum depression. Certainly four-year-old Little Bill couldn't be expected to comprehend his stepmother's vicious words. Sylvia never bothered explaining this and often delighted in Steven's pain when she told stories of how his birth had ruined his mother's life.

Once she'd taken him to the hospital to visit his biological mother. Anita had good days and bad days. Unfortunately for him, the day Sylvia chose for their visit was on one of her bad days. Steven stood next to his mother waiting for her to embrace him, or to at least say hello. Instead, she turned to the expectant ten-year-old and spat on him. He ran from the room and wondered if his stepmother had been right after all.

* * *

It's probable that Sylvia Ipock White eyed the dry cleaners garment bag she'd placed on the living room sofa that summer day in June. She might have recalled stories of small children being suffocated by placing the bags over their heads. Briefly, she wondered how long it would take them to die. Probably no more than a few minutes. Three, maybe four minutes. That wasn't long. Certainly it wasn't as bad as say, bleeding to death, or drowning, or something slow and painful, like poison.

Sylvia was tired of the constant caring her step son required. She'd done the baby thing with her own three sons. She didn't even like Little Bill that much anyway. Everything in her day to day life had to be planned according to his needs. She was tired of it. Sylvia needed more freedom. She observed the plastic dry cleaning bag on the sofa. An idea formed.

All of the boys were at the swimming pool. Billy was at work. Sylvia was glad Teresa no longer lived at home. She didn't know when another opportunity would present itself. She knew it had to be done. It would be over in a few days and she could resume her life, only she would have one less problem to worry about. It would be a piece of cake. It was now or never.

She saw Little Bill sitting on the floor in the living room. "What are you doing?" She said hatefully.

He did not respond.

She yanked the child by his arm, pulling him to a standing position. Sylvia looked at the dry cleaners plastic on the sofa. Without further ado, she grabbed the bag in one hand and continued her hold on Little Bill with the other.

Before she could change her mind, she placed the plastic over Little Bill's head, then shoved him to the floor. She sat on top of him, all the while holding the plastic bag over his head as tight as possible. He strained against the plastic as she tightened her hold. Sylvia counted. One. Two. Three. She couldn't look at the frightened eyes of the child. He struggled, but she was stronger. She pulled the plastic tighter around his neck. After what might have been three or four minutes, Sylvia removed the plastic from the child's head. She released her hold on Little Bill, then tore the bottom half of the bag in half and proceeded to stuff the plastic down the child's throat. She pushed it back as far as she could. She looked down his throat. Nothing. There was nothing to see.

Now, it was time to finish her act.

She grabbed Little Bill's lifeless body and ran outside where she got in her car. She pulled out of the driveway, and once she was a few feet from the house, she began pounding on the horn. Pete Barnes was outside working in his yard. He heard the sound of a car horn blaring. He ran to the edge of his lawn and saw Mrs. White's car stopped in the middle of Hodges road.

"Help me, help me! Please, help me!" Sylvia shouted out the open drivers side window.

Without a second thought, Pete jumped into Mrs. White's vehicle. "Lady, you're in no condition to drive!" They rushed to Lenoir Memorial Hospital's emergency room.

* * *

The White and Ipock boys were getting ready to go home for the afternoon when their neighbor, Tom Chaney, came running up the street to the pool. "There's been an accident."

Curious, they pedaled as fast as they could to find out what the commotion was all about. Hoping to delay bad news, they went into the garage to put their bicycles away when they heard their father's car pull up in the drive. The boys thought this unusual since it was early afternoon and he wasn't due home until later that evening. Sylvia, sobbing uncontrollably, opened the passenger door and ran inside without stopping to speak to them.

"What's wrong?" Steven asked. He went to the rear of the vehicle where his father stood with his head in his hands. He was crying. He'd never seen his father acting so strange before and it scared him. His father was a big man, one Steven thought would never cry, yet here he was right in broad daylight in the front yard crying uncontrollably.

"What is it Dad?" Steven questioned.

His father pinched the bridge of his nose and wiped a tear from his eyes.

"He didn't make it."

Steven was really frightened now. "Who didn't make it? What are you talking about?"

His father quietly sobbed.

"Where is Little Bill? He was here when we left for the pool." Steven persisted and held his breath, knowing, yet not wanting to admit something terrible must have happened.

Steven recalled the time when his brother had burnt himself on the grill in the backyard. It was just a few days ago. He'd been burnt pretty badly, but Sylvia had cleaned his wounds and wrapped them in plastic. *No, it couldn't be that, he thought.* Then he remembered that two weeks earlier he had come home and found his brother just staring at the floor in the living room with his head wrapped in a gauze bandage. He recalled asking him over and over what had happened to his head. The little guy had been extremely reluctant to talk to him that day.

"What happened? Did you fall on the grill again?" Steven teased knowing just how accident-prone he was.

Little Billy White shook his head and continued staring at the floor.

He shook his head a second time.

"Why don't you tell me what happened, little guy?" Steven probed.

"I was felled." The four-year-old explained to his older sibling.

Steven questioned him again. Tears fell from Little

Bill's eyes. He continued to stare at the floor.

"C'mon, you can tell me. I promise I won't tell if you were playing on the grill again."

"I was felled." Little Billy insisted, then looked up at him, pointing toward the stone fireplace.

It only took a minute for Steven to understand what his younger brother was trying to tell him. He'd been pushed.

Steven White was brought back to the present when he saw the tears in his father's eyes.

"Was it from the fall on the fireplace?" Steven asked his father.

Billy White looked at his son as though he could see right through him. It was obvious to Steven that his father had no clue what he'd been referring to.

"No." His father's monotone voice upset him. He wasn't sure if he wanted to know more.

He looked to his father for some sort of assurance; anything to postpone what ten-year-old Steven White knew must be the truth.

Something terrible had happened and he was afraid he knew what it was. Before his father could recite the fateful words, Steven knew Little Bill wouldn't be coming home.

* * *

CHAPTER THREE

When the dust of death has choked
A great man's voice,
the common words he said turn oracles

January 21, 1992

Sylvia White paced back and forth, stopping every few minutes to peer out the front window. It was after midnight and Billy still hadn't returned. It wasn't like him to be this late and not call home. She glanced out the front window again, hoping to see her husband's burgundy Chevy Lumina van in their driveway.

Nothing.

Sylvia went back to her chair and waited, then dozed for a bit, but half listening for Billy's arrival. She slept, then a deep-rooted fear startled her to total wakefulness. She looked at her watch. Daybreak and still no sign of her husband.

Her mind made up, she called the authorities. If it turned out Billy's van had broken down, she figured she was better to be safe than sorry. She would deal with that later. Sylvia called Lenoir County Sheriff's Department and reported her husband missing.

Sylvia explained to the dispatcher that her husband hadn't returned home from a business meeting the previous evening. She said she was terribly concerned because Billy always called if he were going to be delayed. *So far, so good. Everything was going as planned.*

Police officers responded to Sylvia's request to file a missing person's report. As is quite common in a small town, the news of Billy White's disappearance spread fast. The ink on the report was barely dry before others at the sheriff's office got word of the distressing news.

Sheriff Billy Smith and the missing man were good friends. The sheriff had a feeling about his friend's disappearance. Billy White was a loyal family man. The sheriff had no doubt something was wrong. It wasn't like Billy to just up and disappear. Worry gnawed at the sheriff as he raced to the White home. He had a bad feeling about this and didn't like it at all.

All of Kinston's finest raced to the White's recently constructed dream home located at 1909 Eleanor Drive where they found Sylvia worried and on edge. Waiting anxiously for news of her missing husband, she invited the policemen inside.

Sylvia told the officers that her husband had a business appointment scheduled for the previous evening. The meeting was to be in Trenton, a small town about twenty minutes away from Kinston.

She had attended a cosmetic surgery seminar the Monday night before at the Sheraton, she explained. Billy knew of her meeting and had stopped by the motel to tell her that his plans had changed. He gave her a quick goodbye kiss and said he would see her later that evening. Sylvia went home after the seminar and waited for her husband's arrival. Hours went by, but still, there was no sign of him. At dawn, she told the officers that's when she decided to call them to report Billy as a missing person.

News of Billy's disappearance spread fast in the small

town. Just a few weeks before Christmas, the Whites had hosted a housewarming party. Their dream home, a large, pale brick two-story had been filled with joyous laughter from friends and family. A beautifully landscaped lawn, surrounded by professionally trimmed hedges, not to mention its location being one of Kinston's most elite neighborhoods, (according to some) the Whites were considered one of the lucky ones who had "made it."

Now, however, the family home was filled with relatives and friends, shocked that Billy had simply vanished. Well-liked in the community, Billy C. White was a workaholic, and had a proven record as a successful insurance salesman for Jefferson Pilot. His days off were devoted to local charities. He was extremely active in many local civic groups. He also served on the board for a group that provided scholarships for needy students and victims of domestic violence. He was also deeply involved with the local Crimestoppers board, who would offer an eleven-thousand dollar reward for information leading to Billy White's discovery.

Billy was quite popular in Kinston. Not only was he on speaking terms with Ronald Reagan and Jessie Helms, he was also friendly with those that lived in some of Kinston's less desired areas. When forming a search party, the scope of Billy's popularity could be called enormous.

Officers at the house on Eleanor Drive remained behind while Kinston's city and county officials began their search. Sylvia White could hardly function. Normally swift and efficient, she was at a loss since there was nothing she could do about her missing husband. She made herself useful by explaining to the investigators the area where her husband was supposed to meet a new client by the name of Tim Conners. She was sure of the location, she said, because it was she herself who took the message when she'd stopped by her husband's office earlier that day. This wasn't unusual, since she often made appointments for her husband when he was out of the office.

Teresa White-Murray, Billy's oldest daughter, now married with a child of her own, couldn't believe her father had vanished without a trace. One could practically tell the time of day by his routine. At precisely 5:00 P.M., Billy came home. He and Sylvia would have dinner, or occasionally they would dine out. Her father would relax a bit, then spend the remainder of the evening on the phone with his many clients. Teresa thought it odd that her father had gone out so late to meet a client, but said nothing. Worried, but sure there was a reasonable explanation for her father's disappearance, Teresa comforted her stepmother, telling her everything would be just fine.

Little did she know how soon those words would come back to haunt her.

* * *

W. L. Ingram III, known as "Speedy" to his friends and family had worked as Kinston's Assistant Police Chief for nineteen years. He'd been around long enough to know when to listen to his gut instinct and when it was simply another case of indigestion. Today was not a simple case of too much spicy food.

When Speedy had first learned that local businessman and friend Billy White had been reported missing earlier in the day, he was suspicious. It wasn't like Billy to just up and disappear. Several phone calls later, an aerial search was arranged and Sheriff Smith was adamant about assisting the Kinston police in their search. As the sheriff climbed inside the small airplane with Lieutenant Randy Gaskins and Officer Greg Daughtry, he feared what their aerial search might find.

* * *

Major Ingram knew this wasn't going to be a good day when Lieutenant Gaskins lined the small aircraft up with the runway at Kinston's Airport, telling the officers they had just enough fuel for one more go around if they were game for it. They were. The small aircraft turned and made one more attempt before returning to refuel.

As they gave one last look to the logging area below them, they continued to search the pulp wood roads. Through the thick growth of trees they spotted a splash of red. Flying at an altitude of fifteen hundred feet they soon discovered the splash of color they saw through the trees was none other than Billy C. White's missing van. Speedy shifted in his seat and prepared himself for the worst.

On the ground, Detective Ronnie Ingram, along with officers Steven Hockfield and Brooks Bennett waited for further instruction from the plane circling above.

Lieutenant Gaskins radioed the unmarked vehicle. "Ground, do you copy?"

"Go ahead." Replied Detective Ingram.

The aircraft gave their location to the ground officers. Once the vehicle reported they had the plane within sight, Major Ingram instructed the ground officers to visually follow them.

"Do you see a gray vehicle on state road 1156?" Gaskins asked.

"We have the vehicle in sight," said Detective Ingram.

"Continue to follow that car till I tell you to stop."

"Ten-four," from the ground.

The ground officers were directed by the officers in the low flying plane to turn onto a pulp wooded road. The small aircraft continued to circle above them so they could lead them to the area where they'd spied Billy White's missing van.

Once they spotted the van, Detective Ingram proceeded to block the road. Something told him they were about to preserve what might be a possible crime scene.

They inched their way to the van, unsure of what to expect. Detective Ingram arrived at the scene and radioed the plane. Not only had they found the missing van, they'd also discovered the body of Billy C. White at the back of the van lying face up, covered in blood.

* * *

CHAPTER FOUR

Luck is not chance –
It's toil – Fortune's expensive smile
It's earned –.

Valdosta, Georgia
2001

As far as Woodrow "Woody" Taylor is concerned, O.J. Simpson owes him thirty-five-thousand dollars.

For forty-five years Woody Taylor had a story to tell, yet not a single soul would listen to him. Now, however, someone was willing to pay him big bucks for a story he'd told numerous times to friends and family. Sadly, it took a double murder and what police ruled a suicide (this has never been confirmed by an autopsy at the time of this writing) to gain the ear of a listener.

Woody had spoken with an attorney, even hired a big Hollywood agent to negotiate the terms in which he would tell his story. He was making around eighty-thousand dollars a year, didn't really need the money at this point in his life, but he figured after what he'd endured, he deserved compensation. After two weeks of haggling, Woody Taylor's agent and the producers of *Inside Edition* agreed that his story was worth thirty-five-thousand dollars. He was packed and ready to leave for California. However, as fate would have it, another double murder took place that weekend dominating the news.

The bodies of Nicole Brown Simpson, ex-wife of football star O.J. Simpson, and Ronald Goldman, a friend of Nicole's had been found brutally murdered in the plush neighborhood of Brentwood on Bundy Drive.

Woody, along with millions of other viewers stayed glued to his television set as the California Highway Patrol pursued a white Ford Bronco. The producers of *Inside Edition* forgot all about a murder in Kinston. Woody Taylor lost his chance to tell his story because a celebrity's wife and friend were murdered. He figured O.J. was responsible for his lost windfall.

Born and raised in Kinston, Woody Taylor came from a large, hardworking family. The youngest of five, Woody was raised by parents who'd never had an education and wanted to make sure all of their children at least finished high school. He'd also been taught that honesty and hard work were traits that couldn't be bought.

This deep sense of responsibility is what prompted Woody to stay home the summer he was eighteen so he could help his father harvest the last of their tobacco crop. Even though his pals were cruising around town in their hot rods, Woody knew it was his duty to help his father. He didn't mind this, because if it weren't for his father, he would've dropped out of high school and probably turned into a juvenile delinquent. Besides, had he not stayed in school and started playing basketball, he would never have met Sylvia Howard.

Woody would think of her and his heart would pound so fast, he feared it would explode. He recalled the first time he saw her at a high school basketball game in Deep Run. She'd been sitting on the bleachers with her cousin, Shirley. They were playing Pink Hill, their rival. It was his last game of the season. Deep Run was determined to win the championship. They'd played hard for this moment. Woody, co-captain of the team, wanted to end his senior year with a big win.

Naturally, the two girls cheered for Pink Hill. Woody caught the blue-eyed beauty staring at him as he trailed down the court. Shirley jokingly shouted something to him. He couldn't hear what she said, but he paused, saw Sylvia smile at her cousin's remark, then smile at him. In an instant, his heart turned to mush.

For weeks after that last game Woody often wondered about the beautiful young girl who'd made such an impression on him.

After graduating high school, Woody spent the summer helping his father harvest the tobacco crop as promised. That completed and his future staring him squarely in the face, Woody decided to take a job in Kinston working for his older brother. The drive was much too long from Deep Run to Kinston, so it was decided he would move in with his sister Pearl, and brother-in-law Earl Green to their apartment in Kinston.

When Woody discovered the young woman who'd plagued his thoughts for so many weeks was living with her sister and brother-in-law in the upstairs apartment in the same building, Woody thought he had to be the luckiest guy alive.

A few weeks later they started dating. Woody, soon to be nineteen and Sylvia just sixteen, felt a bit wiser than his new girlfriend, but she was definitely the worldlier. He tried on many occasions to find out about her past and her family. Coming from such a large, close-knit family himself, Woody couldn't understand why Sylvia was so hesitant to discuss her own. He knew she'd been raised in an orphanage. She never told him why, but after they'd been dating a while parts of the story spilled forth.

Sylvia was raised in The Kennedy Home, a Baptist children's home in nearby Trenton. He figured she was around five at the time she arrived. He'd never seen her at school dances or anything teens were apt to do, so he figured she must have stayed at The Kennedy Home until she was fifteen or sixteen because he would've remembered a pretty girl like her. He'd picked up bits and pieces about her family and had come up with a background of sorts. At least it was something he could tell his friends and family. He knew her parents were dead and that she had an older sister, Marianna. Somewhere along the line, Marianna met up and married Chilton Howard, who shared the same last name, but was no blood relation to the Howard girls.

Once Sylvia told Woody that her mother had died of an appendicitis attack when she was five. She said her father's grief was so great that he turned to a bottle for comfort. While lapping up the comfort of Jim Beam, and a few of his buddies, he'd neglected the comfort and care of his own daughters. Hence Sylvia's residing at The Kennedy Home. However, Woody wasn't stupid. He knew there was more to the story than that, but he never questioned Sylvia. There was no reason to. He was in love and all was right with the world.

As was bound to happen with two teenagers living in such close proximity without much adult supervision, Woody's and Sylvia's relationship progressed into a sexual one.

For several months the young couple would find a quiet place where they could be alone. They would discuss their hopes and dreams as any couple would, yet Sylvia insisted that they date other people. Woody wasn't comfortable with this. He was in love with Sylvia and didn't need or want anyone else. Heartbroken, Woody took a back seat on those nights when he would visit Sylvia's and discover that she'd just left with another guy.

Sylvia didn't like the rules her sister and brother-in-law had for her. She wanted more freedom to do as she pleased. When she found out her cousin Shirley was in the market for a roommate, she eagerly filled the spot. At first Woody didn't like this new arrangement because he knew it would enable Sylvia to pursue other men. On the other hand, she was still sleeping with him and it did give them more opportunity to be alone.

On one occasion Woody drove over to Sylvia's apartment. They'd had a date set for the evening. When Woody knocked on the door, Shirley, who'd been ironing in the front room acted very strange.

"Where is Sylvia?"

Shirley hem-hawed around with the clothes she was ironing and mumbled, "She's getting ready."

Woody knew the way to her bedroom. He'd been a guest there more than once. He sauntered down the long hall. He opened the door and instead of the scenario he had visualized in his mind, he saw total darkness. He fumbled around the wall searching for the light switch. "Sylvia?" He called into the dark room.

The rustling of covers diverted his attention to the bed. "Are you sick?" He asked the figure lying in the bed.

Surprised, Sylvia said, "No."

Woody realized then that he wasn't the only man in the room, and apparently he wasn't the only man to share her bed.

He stormed out of the apartment swearing he'd never see her again.

Sylvia knew a good thing when she had it and begged Woody to forgive her. She promised she wouldn't see the man again. She told him he was being shipped overseas the next day and she just wanted to make sure he wasn't *the one.* She swore nothing had happened. Woody thought her way of finding *the one* extreme, but he forgave her because he loved her so very much.

With the air cleared between them, Woody and Sylvia began to spend more and more time together. It wasn't long before Sylvia discovered she was pregnant. Woody was upset at first, but then the more he thought about it, the more excited he became. He would have a family of his very own. Then he recalled the night he found Sylvia with another man. Not wanting to, but for his own sake, he asked her if it was possible if the other guy could be the father.

"Of course not!" Sylvia said somewhat indignantly.

"Well, I just wanted to know. You know that time and all."

"Yes, and I want you to forget it." Sylvia insisted.

There was no more talk of paternity.

Sylvia managed to hide her pregnancy well. Girdles were all the rage, so it wasn't unusual for her to be wearing one. Woody begged her to marry him.

"No. I don't want to get married now."

"What about the baby? What do you plan to do about that?" Woody asked.

"Can we talk about something else?"

Woody knew Sylvia. When she made up her mind, there was no changing it. He wished she would tell him what her plans for the future were. She was near five months along and soon she wouldn't be able to hide their baby beneath a panty girdle.

A few weeks later Woody was hanging out with the guys at the drive-in. They were shooting the bull like guys do.

Woody wanted to tell someone of his and Sylvia's predicament, but he'd promised her he wouldn't say anything until she was ready.

His thoughts must have been telepathic that evening.

"Hey, Woody, here comes Chilton," one of his male friends said.

Chilton Howard didn't hang with the guys, at least not that Woody knew of. It couldn't be good news that he'd followed him to the drive-in.

"Hey, you little son of a bitch," Chilton called to Woody.

Sylvia's guardian and brother-in-law, who Woody thought of as a loud mouth and a show off--all talk with no balls--was the center of attention that evening.
He'd just found out that Sylvia was pregnant.

* * *

CHAPTER FIVE

A dead man cannot bite.

January 21, 1992
Approximately 4:00 P.M.

William Kenneth Raper, "Ken" to those who knew him, had been employed by North Carolina's State Bureau of Investigation for nearly fourteen years. His title was that of a Crime Scene Search Specialist. His work took him to ten counties along the coastal areas of North Carolina. His duties were called upon when local police departments needed assistance in processing and examining a crime scene.

It was late afternoon in January when Special Agent Bill Slaughter of the Kinston Police Department contacted Ken. He explained they'd had a murder and his assistance was needed in Jones County.

Around 5:20 P.M., Ken arrived in Jones County where Billy White's body had been found. The scene was sealed with yellow barricade tape. Ken pulled off to the side of the dirt road as ordered by Captain Mike Garrett of Kinston PD. He told Ken to drive down the logging road about two hundred yards; the officers there would assist him.

Ken saw the late model Chevy van, but his eyes immediately went to the body of Billy C. White lying at the right rear of the vehicle. Laying face up with one hand over his chest and the other extended out to the side, he wore a dark blue suit and a white dress shirt. His shirt was covered in blood from two gun shot wounds he'd received in his upper right chest and his lower left side just above his waistline.

Several items were scattered around Billy's body. Ken began the methodical task of bagging and labeling the evidence. The pockets of Billy White's trousers were pulled outward. Approximately five feet above the victim's head Ken saw a shot shell wadding from a shotgun. Ken stooped to the ground and spotted a Jefferson Pilot ink pen on the victim's chest. Billy's glasses lay to the side of his head. Between his left arm and side Ken found a blue pocketknife and a small metal cross. He put them into a plastic bag and marked them as evidence, paying careful attention to state exactly where he found them in reference to the body's location. Ken went about his task while officers from Kinston PD and the Jones County Sheriff's Department prepared themselves for a murder investigation.

* * *

When Steven White received a phone called from a friend of his who had a police scanner and learned that not only had they discovered his father's missing van, but they'd also discovered his father's body lying at the rear of the van, he was shocked.

He placed a call to his sister Teresa White-Murray.

"They found him. He's dead."

Shocked and too upset to drive Teresa's best friend, Cassie Warmack, who was visiting at the time she received the phone call from Steven broke all speed limits driving to the location in Jones County where Teresa's father's van and body had been located. Briefly, Teresa thought of her stepmother and wondered if she'd been told the devastating news.

The days following her father's untimely death were a blur for Teresa. She hardly remembered anything, let alone the minute details that would later become part of a major investigation. She'd lost her father and was having a terrible time dealing with it. At sixteen she'd lost her mother to an institution. Not long after that, her little brother had died a strange death and now this. It was too much to bear.

Teresa's father was a peaceful man. She couldn't imagine someone wanting him dead. Kinston police had no clues in her father's death, or if they did, they weren't sharing them with the family.

Her stepmother was not handling the loss well either. Just days after her father's death, Teresa had been visiting Sylvia. She'd acted strange. Teresa put it down to grief. She knew what it was like. Grief had a funny way of making you do things you normally wouldn't even consider. She assumed that was why on the afternoon of her visit when she observed her stepmother as she invited a long-haired scraggly-looking man into her kitchen--something she would normally not even consider--Teresa knew her stepmother wasn't in her right mind.

Later she would recall this event. Its reason would be earth shattering.

* * *

CHAPTER SIX

To fight aloud is very brave,
But gallant, I know,
Who charge within the bosom
The cavalry of woe.

May, 1954

It didn't take much persuasion to convince Woody to marry Sylvia. He'd been after her for months to do the right thing and he was pissed that it had come down to this. He didn't like how Chilton made him feel like a loser, an irresponsible jerk. He tried explaining this to his future brother-in-law.

"I've been trying to get Sylvia to tell ya'll for months now. She said she wasn't ready to get married." Woody said.

"Well, let me assure you she's ready now. She's at the house. Now, go on over there, she's waiting."

Woody had no clue what he could do this late at night, but he sure as hell wasn't going to tell that to Chilton now. There'd be time for further explanations later. He hoped he finally had his wish. Even though his marriage to Sylvia wasn't going to take place under the circumstances he would've liked, it *was* going to happen and for now, that's what mattered most.

With all of his buddies as witnesses to the event that was sure to be the talk of the town tomorrow, Woody could barely hear his own words when he spoke. "I need to take these guys home first. They rode with me."

"They can hitch hike, I don't give a damn what they do, but your ass is going to get Sylvia right now."

Chilton didn't mince words. Woody knew he meant what he said. He'd never cared too much for the man simply because Woody thought him as nothing more than a big blast of hot air, but he was Sylvia's guardian and he respected him for that reason alone.

He looked over his shoulder at his pals, trying to appear as casual as he could. "Hey guys, good luck getting home. See ya 'll later."

Woody drove the short distance to Marianna and Chilton's apartment. A thousand thoughts swirled through his mind. Was he doing the right thing? He was going to be a father. What could possibly be wrong? He loved Sylvia passionately. A cloud of doubt shadowed his elation. Did she love him? She hadn't actually said the words, but he'd assumed she had. They'd been intimate, for Pete's sake. Of course she loved him. What sort of girl would let a man make love to her if she wasn't in love with him? Briefly, Woody remembered the night he'd found Sylvia in bed, making sure the other man wasn't *the one.* He pushed the thought aside. It wouldn't do him a bit of good to dwell on the past.

Woody hurriedly went to the downstairs apartment where he lived with his sister, threw his clothes in a suitcase, and saw that Sylvia was waiting for him outside while he loaded the trunk.

It was almost eight o'clock. He hadn't a clue what he could accomplish this late at night, but Sylvia got in the car and they drove straight to Dylan, South Carolina. Once there, they found themselves a cheap motel room and spent the night before their wedding discussing the future.

Early the next morning the young couple drove through the town in search of a Justice of the Peace. Once located, they were quickly married, then on their way home to begin their lives as a couple.

Fortunately Woody had a very good job working for his older brother and was able to care for his new wife without help from anyone. They rented a house, went to Sears and Roebuck where they did, as any other young married couple would be expected to do, and bought a houseful of furniture on credit.

Though Woody was gainfully employed, he still had no health insurance and now with a baby on the way he needed insurance, and a lot more. By mutual agreement with his brother, they decided he would work fifteen-hour days to make extra money for the hospital bill and a little to tuck away, just in case.

On September 17, 1954, Sylvia gave birth to a healthy son. They named him Jeff. Woody couldn't have been happier.

Working six days a week, sometimes as many as sixteen hours a day didn't give him much time to spend with his new family. But that's how it had to be, Woody told himself. It was his responsibility to take care of his wife and son, even if it meant not seeing them as much as he would've liked. It never occurred to him that spending so much time working would cause problems. He had a family now and it was his duty to provide for them. Given the way he was brought up, there was absolutely no possibility of his family ever depending on welfare or public assistance of any kind. It just didn't happen in the Taylor family.

One particular evening Woody came home from work earlier than usual. Sylvia was in the kitchen located at the back of the house and didn't hear him enter. He was quiet when he came in, not to be sneaky; he just never knew when his son might be napping. Upon entering the living room Woody stopped when he saw a letter propped up on the coffee table. Possibly Sylvia had forgotten to put it out in the mail. He reached for the letter and stopped cold in his tracks when he saw the name on the envelope.

Sylvia must have heard him then because she tore into the front room, rage contorting her features. "What are you doing?" She shouted and tried to grab the letter from him.

"I think I should be asking you that question." Woody stared at her. She looked right through him. Her stare was so cold he shivered. He'd never seen her look at him that way. It frightened him. This was not the girl he'd married.

Before he knew what was happening, Sylvia attacked him, trying to tear the letter from his grasp. She clawed at him with her nails, anything to snatch the letter from his grasp. She wasn't strong enough. Woody took the letter and left the house. He drove down the block, pulled off to the side of the road and read the contents. Expecting anything but what he read, he fumed as he read the words. It was to *him*, the guy from the army. *The one.* He skimmed the letter. One sentence caught his eye. *I wish the baby had been yours.*

Now he had no doubt Jeff was his son.

Woody began to have doubts about everything else in his life. Their marriage was a lie. If Sylvia continued to write love letters to the man she wished had fathered their son, were there more men he didn't know about? Hating to admit it, even to himself, he was afraid he'd made a mistake by marrying Sylvia, but he loved her so much. He had to forgive her. She'd been young when they married and didn't have much of an opportunity to date. No wonder she was still writing schoolgirl letters.

For the time being, things were back to normal in the Taylor household. Woody continued to work long hours while Sylvia took care of their son and home.

* * *

Married life wasn't all that exciting for Sylvia. She would pick fights with Woody for lack of anything better to do. This went on for almost a year. Woody tried everything he knew to make his wife happy. She wasn't very materialistic, so he didn't feel he needed to "buy" her affection, but there was something about her that wasn't quite right.

At times Sylvia could be the sweetest woman in the world. Then there were the times he wished he could forget. Sylvia had a terrible temper. Usually Woody never had a clue why his young wife was so angry. She would attack him, hitting him with her fists, tearing his clothes, scratching, clawing and swinging at him. Her eyes would glass over, possibly with an inner fury known only to her. Then, as fast as the fits of rage would begin, they would end. Sylvia was back to her old self and all was forgotten. Even an apology.

Woody wasn't sure how much more he could tolerate. While he wanted his marriage to succeed, he didn't know if it was worth the price Sylvia asked. Hating to admit defeat, Woody knew it was for the best to end his marriage. He left Sylvia and Jeff, yet continued to provide for them. Marianna, concerned that her sister was left with a toddler to rear on her own, plus she really liked Woody, made a decision.

"Woody, give Sylvia another try. I don't know why she acts the way she does, but she's promised me she would change."

Still in love with her, he knew he had to give his marriage a second chance.

Back at home, Woody was amazed at how sweet and kind Sylvia acted. But that was it. It had all been an act so that he would return. After two weeks of playing the role of good wife, Sylvia resorted back to her mean ways and again, he left in order to preserve his sanity.

Over the next year, Woody would move in and out of their home at least a half- dozen times. He was concerned at what effect this had on Jeff, but the child never seemed to notice, yet he was still a toddler and Woody knew Jeff wasn't aware of the state of their marriage. Sylvia took good care of Jeff, and Woody gave her credit for that. She never lashed out at him, never lost her temper. She was a good mother; at least he didn't have to worry about Jeff.

However, Sylvia didn't like the loss of control. She wanted Woody at her beck and call. Many times throughout the first year of their separation she would call Woody trying to coax him over to her house.

"Jeff is sick. I need you to come over." Woody received many calls like this at work and at home. Being a good father and wanting to do all that he could for his son, he went to Sylvia's whenever possible. More often than not, there wasn't anything wrong with Jeff. Sylvia would then explain that she just wanted to see him.

Woody had enough of her games. He filed for a legal separation, knowing this was the only way he could get on with his life. At that time in the state of North Carolina a couple who filed for a legal separation were not to contact one another for one year. If there was contact, then the date of the legal separation began all over again from the date of the last encounter.

Sylvia learned of this through a savvy new girlfriend and delighted in torturing Woody this way. She would lure

Woody over on the pretext that Jeff was ill, making sure there was a witness to the meeting. Then their legal separation would drag on for another year. This amused her.

On one such occasion Woody received a telephone call from Sylvia crying frantically. “Please Woody, you’ve got to come. It’s Jeff. He’s been electrocuted. I’ve got to get him to the hospital.”

Knowing this was just another ploy to get him to come to her house, he didn’t go. He’d been fooled one time too many.

Later he would learn that Sylvia had been ironing. Instead of unplugging the iron from the wall outlet, she’d unplugged the cord from the base of the iron. Apparently, Jeff had grabbed the cord and stuck in down his throat.

Years later this event would be recalled from none other than Jeff himself. His memory of events and those of his mother were quite different.

* * *

CHAPTER SEVEN

The belief in a supernatural source of evil is not necessary, men alone are quite capable of every wickedness.

Deep Run, North Carolina

Sylvia Howard Taylor Ipock White's early beginnings remain somewhat of a mystery. Though clouded with rumors and innuendos, no one really knows the truth. If they do, they're either dead or prefer to remain silent. I believe it to be a combination of both.

Some believe Sylvia witnessed a terrible tragedy before she was sent to live at The Kennedy Home in Trenton, creating future behavior that was inevitable. Others believe her inclination for violence started at the moment of conception.

Located fifteen miles south of Kinston is the small farming community of Deep Run. During the Civil War Deep Run was called Red Town because all of the homes and buildings were painted red. With a population somewhere between two and three hundred, they boasted a post office, their own fire department and South Lenoir High School. They had one grocery store, two churches and a café. Home of former North Carolina Senator, Harold Hardison, Deep Run is a sleepy little community where families have lived off the land for generations.

In such a small rural area everyone knew everyone

else, plus a bit of their business whether they wanted them to or not. Rumors spread like wildfire and local gossip mongers fed heartily on this.

Bob Deaver grew up in Deep Run. He recalled a time from his youth when he was so terrified it would become his most horrifying childhood memory.

Terry Tyndall, a long time resident of Deep Run was known as the meanest man around. Cold-hearted and ruthless, those that knew him wished they didn't. Known for his cruelty toward women, both married and single led him to spend several years in prison for attempted murder. (I tried to locate Terry Tyndall's prison files. This was fruitless because in the 1920's when it is believed that Terry Tyndall served time, I could not validate this since record keeping didn't begin until the 1930's. His criminal history has not been documented as of this writing).

According to Bob Deaver, who heard the story from a long-time Deep Run resident, Tyndall walked everywhere he went. On one of his daily excursions Tyndall was picked up by a wealthy landowner passing by in his horse and carriage. The landowner was accompanied by his wife. He offered to give Tyndall a ride into town. During the ride Tyndall began to fondle the landowner's wife. When his wife told her husband of this just minutes after it happened the landowner (who remains nameless to this day) defended his wife. For this, Tyndall nearly stabbed him to death. Though he never carried a gun, he knew how to yield a knife and literally put the fear of God in all that had the misfortune to come in contact with him.

Bob recalled a time as a young boy when he was at the local general store. The door flew open and a man winded from running, shouted to the patrons inside. "Terry Tyndall is coming!"

The store owner flew into a panic. The door burst open with Tyndall blocking the doorway so there was no chance of escape.

"I'm sorry, please . . . It was an accident." The store owner begged. "I didn't see you. It was dark. I never meant to run you off the road!"

Deavers is sure he had never seen a grown man more frightened. He was also sure he that was about to witness a murder.

After much begging and pleading, Tyndall apparently decided the store owner wasn't worth killing and allowed him live. Deavers would later think back on this event and realize just what a psycho Terry Tyndall was.

Knowing Tyndall's tendency toward violence, one can only assume it likely that any offspring of his would be predisposed to erratic behavior also.

In Deep Run there are those who believe Sylvia's origins are a product of an unholy union between her mother and Terry Tyndall. Some believe Tyndall raped Mrs. Howard, while others believe they may have had an affair. Given his history with women, rape is a high probability. It would explain Sylvia's mental status. Then there are those who are sure Sylvia witnessed her mother's murder at the tender age of five. Some say her father murdered his wife in a drunken fit of rage. Could it be he discovered his wife's affair with Tyndall? Was Sylvia a witness to her mother's death? One will never know. However, Sylvia's future behavior would dictate that one of these stories must be true.

* * *

CHAPTER EIGHT

Every day is a fresh beginning,
Every morn is the world made new.

Sylvia Howard Taylor was single again. Even though she'd done everything thing in her power to delay her impending divorce, she'd failed. Disliking the loss of control made her angry. In the past she'd simply pitched a fit and gotten her way. When that didn't work, she could always find something wrong with Jeff. She must've lost her touch because Woody wanted nothing more to do with her. As much as she hated to admit defeat, she eventually chalked her failed marriage down to Woody's loss. There were more fish in the sea. She had the bait; she just needed the right hook.

Woody kept his promise and paid regular child support for Jeff. It wasn't long after her separation from Woody when Sylvia learned that Chilton wanted to buy her half of some farmland that was left to her and Marianna when their father died. Thinking this a dream come true, she sold her half of the property, collected a hefty forty-thousand dollars and went on with her life. She purchased a fancy new car and would often be seen driving around town with Jeff standing up in the front seat.

It may have been on one of these drives that Sylvia met Leslie Ipock. Handsome, single and susceptible to Sylvia's charm, the two became an item. On May 23, 1959 they made it official by getting married.

Leslie's family treasured his new bride. She was sweet, funny and their brother was in love. With nine children in the Ipock family, one would think when one left home to marry they wouldn't be missed too much. This was not the case with Leslie Ipock. Very close and much loved by his family, after marrying Sylvia he continued to visit his mother, father and siblings. Sylvia, on the other hand could not understand for the life of her why her husband had to visit his mother all the time. Certainly one would not call Leslie Ipock a "mama's boy" but one could call him a devoted and loving son. Whenever possible he would stop by his parents' house just so he could have a cup of his mother's coffee that he was so fond of. This angered Sylvia so much that she asked him to stop the constant visits.

"Why would I do that?' Leslie inquired of his young wife.

"Because I don't like it. You should be here with me where you belong." Sylvia told him, her tone that of a sulking child.

Sylvia and Leslie had just spent the day with his family last Sunday, Leslie thought she seemed fine at the time. But knowing Sylvia as he did, someone could have said something she didn't like and this was her way of making him pay for it.

"Don't you think that's being unreasonable?"

"Not at all. I'm your wife. It's my right." Leslie could tell by her tone the topic was closed. He let it slide. He'd see mama next week and ask her what had been said that might have upset his wife. Most likely nothing.

* * *

CHAPTER NINE

It's a mad world. Mad as Bedlam.

January 22, 1992

The Free Press' headlines read: *MISSING INSURANCE AGENT FOUND MURDERED.*

The small community of Kinston was shocked. How could this happen to one of the most prominent citizens in town? People were frightened. This had been the second murder of an insurance salesman in Lenoir County in seven weeks.

Jasper Lee Albritton had been found shot execution style in his home just weeks before. Those who had the slightest connection to anything related to the insurance world were terrified. Could an unhappy client with an insurance transaction gone bad set out for revenge? Or, were these random killings and it mere coincidence that both victims happened to sell insurance?

Detective Lieutenant Randy Askew either wasn't saying, or simply did not know. Evidence wasn't overflowing at this point, but he did have proof of something: Billy White was alone when he drove out to the logging road. However, tire tracks suggested he may have been followed. Askew admitted to the press that while numerous vehicles had been down the road, he wasn't one-hundred percent sure if there was a connection to Billy White or his death.

Though they weren't coming up empty-handed, police couldn't connect the physical evidence at the scene of the crime to a possible motive or suspect.

Not yet.

Henry Poole, an agent with the State Bureau of Investigation told reporters, "There's no way to tell if it was a set up."

The White family was in a state of shock. Sylvia, now Billy's widow told officers again about her husband's meeting with prospective client Tim Conner. Family members were questioned about this meeting. Still nothing. However, Teresa White-Murray had a hard time imagining her father driving to Jones County to an abandoned logging road, especially that late in the evening. It was wintertime. The sun set early and her father had suffered a life-long fear of the dark. It did not compute.

Tony Ipock, Sylvia's eldest son knew of the meeting his stepfather had planned with this new client. "He had never met the client before. He had talked to him on the phone several times."

This statement in itself aroused suspicion. Mrs. White claimed to have spoken with this client herself making all the arrangements. Nothing was ever mentioned about Billy White speaking with him, nor was any indication given that Tony was aware of the meeting. Police officials were stumped. Why would Tony Ipock, a hairdresser at the *Polished Act* know so much about his stepfather's comings and goings when Billy's own children knew virtually nothing? Were they on to something?

As the saying goes, talk is cheap. In this case however, talk would turn out to be priceless for the Kinston PD and the

SBI (State Bureau of Investigation).

Word has it the day of Billy White's disappearance while pictures of him were flashing over television sets across the county, Tim Jones sat in a local bar telling his drinking partner how he'd been asked to murder Mr. White. He said he'd been given a picture of him and a few particulars, but nothing ever came of it. He'd wanted big bucks up front and apparently the wife couldn't get her hands on any cash until *after* the murder.

News travels fast, especially bad news and Kinston was no different. It wasn't long before Kinston PD and the SBI heard this information from a confidential informant.

"I think I might know what happened to Billy White," The informant told authorities.

After receiving an unexpected tip made to the local Crimestoppers hotline, local law enforcement officials weren't sure if they had a possible suspect, or if this was just another one of many crank calls. They hoped this was a starting point and the evidence would mount up so they could solve the case. Billy was friendly with everybody in town. Cries for an arrest were coming from all walks of life.

* * *

CHAPTER TEN

This learned I from the
shadow of a tree,
That to and fro did sway against
a wall,
Our shadow selves, our influence may fall
Where we ourselves can never be.

James Lynwood Taylor was born and raised in Lenoir County. The eldest of four, Lynwood's life as a youngster appeared relatively normal to outsiders. He attended church as a child with his siblings. Always obedient and helpful to others, he was known as a good boy to family and friends.

Taylor's educational life was a different matter. Handicapped with a speech impediment, he had difficulty in school. Learning was hard for him. He'd had to repeat the first grade and he felt this was a reflection on him. He didn't feel worthy, and felt he deserved to fall short.

In high school, it was more of the same. Though Taylor's grades were marginal, he managed to graduate from North Lenoir High School in 1972 with the sixteen units required to earn a high school diploma. Upon graduation, he married his high school sweetheart Dianne. Soon after they had a son.

Taylor entered a pre-service enlistment program following graduation. On October 5, 1972 Taylor enlisted in the Air Force for four years. After entering the service, Taylor upped his agreement to six years so it would enable him to attend certain schools.

After receiving his basic training in Texas, Taylor was transferred to Chanute Air Base in Illinois for technical school where he would study heating and air conditioning. Taylor sent for his wife and son, and upon completion of his training was transferred to the air base in Myrtle Beach, South Carolina.

Barely four months had passed when Taylor checked himself into the Air Force Mental Health Center. Diagnosed with depression, he complained of marital problems and said he was having a difficult time functioning in his everyday life.

His psychiatric report read, "*He has problems with his nerves, is upset easily . . . is characterized by helplessness and indecisiveness with a recurrent necessity to have decisions made for him by others. He experiences anxiety especially when there is no strong figure to support him on a continued and day to day basis . . . his character and behavior of passive-dependent personality render him incapable of performing meaningful in the Air Force. . . he has difficulty planning ahead . . . no real planning in education or career . . . talks of inability to cope with life . . . indecisiveness . . . (he) would be viewed as a passive-dependent personality. . . established . . . excessively dependent relationship as had with parents . . . anxiety when there is no strong figure. . .*

Unable to cope with the responsibilities of adulthood, Taylor regressed. He began acting childlike, taking risks that a normal man of his age would never even consider. He drove his motorcycle recklessly. He would go out and party without his wife. Add alcohol, acid, quaaludes and cocaine, and the mixture was explosive.

Dianne made several appointments for her husband at

the Mental Health Center hoping she could intervene and help him with his ongoing problems . . . anything to stop his drug use and wild, childish behavior. He would go once or twice, then stop. He always talked of being depressed. On one occasion he had a gun in the house and he took it with him into the woods. When he finally returned home, he told of his plan to commit suicide, but said he just couldn't do it. Later he was prescribed an antidepressant, but only took it briefly.

Taylor was going through major changes at this point in his life. He feared getting older. Dianne thought this was the reason for his reckless behavior. When his sister called on his thirty-eighth birthday to wish him "happy birthday" he cried. He started hanging out with his son's younger friends, even though this angered his son.

Taylor and Dianne separated in 1991, but continued to see one another on week-ends. Dianne was told he had started seeing other woman and that he was acting even stranger than she could imagine. She said that Taylor was always good to her and gave her everything. They were separated now, so there wasn't anything she could do.

During the course of his treatment, Taylor told of how he'd been sexually molested by his father's youngest brother, Henry Spense. His sisters were also abused by their uncle. Taylor had bad dreams about his uncle for many years because of the abuse.

Billy W. Royal, M.D., a forensic and general psychiatrist summed up Taylor's mental status: "*Mr. Taylor was a rather odd looking person with a prominent chronic skin condition noted on his face. He was pleasant, serious and responsive. His speech was difficult to understand at intervals and he was asked to repeat comments and responses. Problems with memory were noted as to specifics about many of his life experiences. His affect was in general appropriate. He often appeared depressed and on several occasions became emotional, tearful and unable to talk. His comments indicated a poor and confused self-image. Intelligence appears to be in the low/normal range. However, there was a major lack of insight into himself, his behaviors and his relationships as well as a lack of insight into his family. Judgment was seen as marginal. Mr. Taylor had difficulty and inconsistent with the standard mental health questions. He was able to name the current president and vice-president and the states that touch North Carolina. However, he could not name any North Carolina Governors except Governor Hunt. He was unable to continue serial sevens. Unusual responses to Proverbs were given with one indicative of his obsession with aging and death."*

Dr. Royal's diagnostic Impression:

Substance abuse and dependency. IE: Cocaine, alcohol and Valium.

Depression, Major.

Post Traumatic Stress Disorder Secondary to Sexual abuse.

Organic Brain Syndrome. (Provisional)

Personality Disorder.

Dr. Royal commented, "*As noted by various diagnoses Mr. Taylor has several etiological factors that converge to result in the person he is today. The two primary factors that have contributed to his psychological status and his behaviors are: 1. the family lifestyle and relationships and 2. the sexual abuse inflicted on Mr. Taylor as a child.*

These factors have contributed to his being unable to develop a strong, stable male identity and self-image.

Substance dependency with cocaine and other drugs and an inability to set goals, concerns about the future with life as seen as passing him by, have been accompanied by despair, depression and untoward behaviors. Mr. Taylor's inability to seek or accept help, as has been evident by other members of his family, have compounded his problems."

Given his background, James Lynwood Taylor was the perfect person to do the ungodly act that was asked of him. After the death of his mother, his life would form a pattern. Not having much of a relationship with his father had left Lynwood vulnerable and needy. Possibly the attention he craved and so desperately wanted is what put him in a situation where no matter how wrong he thought of what he was being asked to do, with his personality, it was almost a given that this weak and needy man would comply.

Though police still hadn't made an arrest at this point, and were not telling if one was imminent, they knew Billy White's death wasn't a random killing. It had been planned a long time ago.

* * *

CHAPTER ELEVEN

Wide is the gate, and broad is the way,
that leadeth to destruction.

February 12, 1992

James Lynwood Taylor jumped when he heard the shrill ring of the telephone. He'd just finished snorting a few lines of Coke and was trying to relax.

He answered the phone, "Yeah?"

"Is this Lynwood Taylor?" The voice inquired.

"It's me."

"This is Officer Gosnell. I got a couple men down here at the sheriff's office from Duplin County wantin' to talk to you. You got any problem with that?"

Taylor looked around the house, spying the bag of cocaine on the end table. "No, uh, I got no problem with that."

"Get on down here now." Gosnell ordered.

"Be right there."

Taylor fixed another line, inhaled it and quickly ran through his house, picking up things, putting a bit of order to the clutter. He had a weird feeling. He wasn't sure, but something told him he might be out for a while. He played with his dog for a few minutes, then gave a last minute inspection of the house. Everything looked as it should.

Without glancing back, Taylor drove to the sheriff's office wondering if Officer Gosnell wanted some information for another drug bust. Taylor grinned to himself. If they only knew. He'd been working as informant for the Lenoir County Sheriff's Department the past nine or ten months. It was almost better than having a real job. While he turned his friends and enemies in for dealing in drugs, he was also buying and selling. Of course the sheriff's department didn't know this. If they had, he'd been locked up for sure a long time ago. Maybe his luck was runnin' out and someone had seen him in the midst of a deal. No, they wouldn't have called him to come down to the office for that. They would have driven to his place and arrested him. He had an idea of what they might want and hoped he was wrong.

Taylor parked in the lot behind the courthouse where the sheriff's department was located downstairs in the basement. He'd walked this path many times before while working as an informant.

Lester Gosnell saw Taylor as he walked down the hall. "In here." He gestured with his head.

Taylor looked at the men seated in Gosnell's office. Any thought of turning around and walking out the door was just that, a thought.

"Taylor, this is Eric Smith. He's with the SBI. Bennett Sims, and Bill Slaughter, Kinston PD."

Taylor nodded at the three officers. "Hey."

"Mr. Taylor, do you know why we've asked you here?" Eric Smith asked.

Taylor shook his head. "No, sir."

"You know anything about the Billy White case?"

Taylor felt his heart slam against his chest, pounding

so hard he thought it might explode. He wished he hadn't snorted those last few lines of coke.

"Only what's been on the news." Taylor responded.

"You sure about that?" Smith quizzed.

Right now he wasn't going to admit to anything. He didn't know what they knew, or if they knew anything at all. "I'm sure."

"Word has it you know something, Taylor. Why don't you just fess up and be done with it? Mrs. White has told us plenty," Agent Smith said.

"She didn't have anything to do with it." Taylor said, then realized he'd said more than he'd intended.

"And how is it you know this information? I don't think it's been on the news? Has it?"

Smith looked to the other officers in the room for confirmation. They shook their heads indicating it hadn't.

"I just think she didn't that's all. Just my opinion." Taylor suddenly felt a fool, as though he'd been used. He'd *allowed* himself to be used. He was stupid; but he wasn't so stupid that he didn't realize he'd just fallen into the trap that had been set for him.

The men in the room looked at one another, then shifted their gaze to Taylor. They could tell he was uncomfortable. They took this as a sign to become more aggressive in their questions.

"I'll take a polygraph test." Taylor suddenly volunteered.

The three men looked at one another. "We can arrange that."

Without further ado, Eric Smith and the two KPD officers made arrangements for James Lynwood Taylor to take a lie detector test. This could turn their investigation around one way or another and they knew it. They hoped it was in the direction they wanted. If not, they were back to square one.

* * *

Given the amounts of cocaine he'd snorted earlier, plus his general feeling that he could outwit the polygraph, after all it was only a machine. Taylor waited patiently as the machine was being hooked up. The police had left the room, Eric Smith following them. It was just him and the examiner. Taylor felt sure this man wasn't privy to what had transpired between him and those involved.

After the initial base questions to establish the validity of the yes and no questions, the examiner began his questioning.

"Were you involved in the murder of Billy White?"

"No." Taylor responded.

"Was Sylvia White involved in the murder of Billy White?"

"No."

The questions went on for more than an hour. Taylor was getting tired and he was starting to feel nervous. The drugs had long since worn off, and his conscience was starting to nag him.

The examiner removed the wires from him and left the room. Taylor didn't care about the results. He knew what was true and what wasn't. And right now, his conscience was kicking in big time.

"I want to talk to the police again," Taylor informed an officer.

"Sure."

* * *

CHAPTER TWELVE

You can never plan the future by the past.

Spring 1991

"We're having trouble with the windows at the new house," Sylvia White told her son Tony. "Do you know of someone that might be able to come over and take a look at them?"

Knowing his mother as he did, he was sure her question meant something other than what someone else would interpret. Tony Ipock knew lots of people. Though she didn't say the exact words, he knew what sort of person his mother was looking for. "I think I know of someone." Tony told Sylvia.

Sylvia hoped Tony could help her with her problem. Things weren't going well in her life at this point and the last thing she needed was for him to fumble something up as simple as a request. They'd agreed she would come to the *Polished Act* mid-morning the next day.

Sylvia stopped by her son's shop.

About that time the door opened and in walked James Lynwood Taylor.

"Hey, Tony." Taylor said.

Tony turned to his mother who was standing next to

him. "Mother, this is Lynwood Taylor, the man I've been telling you about."

"It's nice to meet you Mr. Taylor," Sylvia shook hands with the long haired man. "I understand you're a carpenter."

"Yes, Ma'am." Taylor replied.

"Could you possibly stop by my house tomorrow morning and look at my windows? We've had some trouble with the framing."

"I reckon I could do that. First thing in the mornin'?"

Though his words weren't perfectly clear, Sylvia understood exactly what Lynwood said.

"Yes, Mr. Taylor, first thing in the morning."

The next morning James Lynwood Taylor arrived at the White home on Roseanne Drive as instructed. He parked his truck in front of the house. Reaching on the seat for some paper, a pencil and a measuring tape, he was surprised to see Mrs. White racing toward his truck.

She carried a fistful of papers in her hand. She looked around at the activity going on behind her. Apparently all the workers were where they were supposed to be. "I know you're going to think I'm crazy, but I'm looking for somebody to kill my husband."

Taylor was flabbergasted. This was the last thing he expected to hear coming from the mouth of this little old lady. Hell, she was a grandma. He knew that because he knew Tony had a kid. Damn! "I'm not the person you need to be talking to about this. I came here to see about a window."

Mrs. White appeared fragile to Mr. Taylor. Tears pooled in her eyes and she became very upset. "I don't why, but I feel as though I can trust you, Mr. Taylor."

"Lady I am *not* the person you're looking for." Taylor

was about to turn and get inside his truck when Sylvia reached out and grabbed him by the arm. "Please, you've got to help me. My marriage is terrible. Billy is a sick pervert. If only you knew. Look." Sylvia held out the papers she clutched in her hand. "See this proves I'm serious. I want you to know just how serious I am. I have some pages here from a book. I went to the library and found a book on poisonous plants found in North Carolina."

Taylor looked at the papers she held out but did nothing.

"I've walked up and down the highway picking up . . . looking for plants. I'd take them home and cook them and put them in his food hoping to poison him and nothing has any effect on him." She sobbed.

Again Sylvia thrust the papers out for Taylor to see. He could tell the pages had been torn from a book.

"I think you need to get professional help. There are people that can help you with this sort of thing. Doncha think killin' your husbands' a bit drastic?" Taylor asked.

Sylvia shook her head from side to side. "If he knew I was standing here talking to you right now he would kill me. I can't let him know anything about this. Please don't tell anybody." Sylvia pleaded to Taylor.

Taylor nodded his reply and asked, "What about the window?"

"I just wanted you to come by here. We'd better make it look real. Come on inside."

Taylor followed Mrs. White into the house, figuring she was whacked out or something. He reckoned she'd forget about killin' her husband and go on with her life.

Together, they walked through the home that would be

Billy and Sylvia White's dream house. Taylor took notes just in case.

He'd remember this day as being one of the strangest in his life.

* * *

CHAPTER THIRTEEN

Look in my face: my name is
Might-have-been;
I am also called No-more, Too late, Farewell

December, 1991

James Lynwood Taylor regretted the day he'd ever laid eyes on Sylvia White. She'd stormed into his life like a raging hurricane and hadn't eased off at all. It'd been a year since she'd first approached him with her plan.

Taylor had told his Uncle, Ernest Basden about Sylvia. "You're not going to believe this, but she's trying to find someone to kill her husband." Basden advised Taylor to stay away from her because she sounded like she was crazy. "I really think she's serious. Says she's going to do it herself." Again, Basden warned his nephew. But the constant phone calls from the woman made it impossible for Taylor to ignore her and he told this to his uncle.

He repeated her last telephone call to his uncle.

"Taylor, we've got to meet. I can't stand it anymore. I don't know what to do."

As always, he let Sylvia say whatever it was that needed to be said before he would speak. "Look, Mrs. White, I got problems of my own."

"I'm sure. But they're not like mine. I can't take it anymore!"

"Listen, calm down. It can't be that bad. Maybe you should think about getting a gun to protect yourself." Taylor always tried to reassure the older woman, but it never seemed to work.

She gave a short laugh. "No! If you only knew. Look, we have to talk. I can't stay on the phone much longer. He could walk in and overhear me."

"I can't . . . "

"Listen to me . . . I'm really, please just meet with me. If you can't help me, then I'm going to kill him myself, then commit suicide! I can't go on like this any longer!" She sobbed hysterically into the phone.

Taylor sighed into the phone. "Maybe you should do it yourself. Make it look like a suicide."

"That's out of the question, my second husband . . . just meet me at the Food Lion Parking lot around eleven." Sylvia hung up the phone, not giving Taylor a chance to answer.

"Who was that?" Dianne asked.

"Nobody."

"Nobody? You spend five minutes on the phone and you want me to believe it's *nobody.* You can't fool me. Who was she?" Dianne persisted.

Taylor had been having an affair and Dianne had recently found out. He'd promised her it was over and it was, but she still didn't trust him. He didn't blame her.

"I gotta go out for a while."

"Where? To meet *her*?"

"No, Dianne. I told you that was over. This is

business."

"Then I'm going with you."

"If that's what you want." Taylor relented.

Not exactly a shopping center or a mall, Food Lion, a southern grocery store chain, was located on Highway 70 in a large lot surrounded by several smaller stores that connected to the building.

Taylor wanted to get this over with as soon as possible. He was tired of dealing with Mrs. White. He wanted to get his life back to normal and so far, nothing he'd achieved even came close to normal. With Sylvia White in the picture, Taylor wasn't sure if there'd ever be any normalcy to his life. Surely, he thought, she wasn't serious. After all this time, maybe she had a crush on him. Maybe she wanted a sexual relationship. He'd caught that from her a time or two and overlooked it. She was married and way too old for him. Definitely not his type. Maybe she wanted something more and was just using this "murder" plot to entice him further, but he didn't know what she could possibly ask of him that could top murder.

He recalled his Uncle Ernest's words. "You'd better stay away from that woman. She's crazy."

Both would remember that foreboding statement for the rest of the natural lives.

* * *

CHAPTER FOURTEEN

Cowards do not count in battle; they are there, but not in it.

"No Ma'am, I cannot do it! There is no way I can take another man's life," Taylor told Sylvia White.

"It's . . . it's not that hard to do. I had a step child once. I put a bag over it until it stopped breathing." Sylvia paused then continued. "It was better off."

Taylor was astounded by Sylvia's confession. It had gone far enough. He couldn't take much more of her. When he responded, his answer surprised him. "Okay, I know someone who will do this. For a price."

Taylor observed the relief etched all over Sylvia White's face. Maybe her husband *was* beating her and making her do all sorts of weird sexual acts.

Sylvia then reached inside her purse and removed a sheet of paper with a map drawn on it. "That won't be a problem. You'll need this."

Even though Taylor had discussed the murder-for-hire plan with his Uncle Ernest at least three times, he was somewhat shocked that he'd just agreed to hire a hit-man for Sylvia White. Time was running out according to her. She wanted the murder to take place right away. She wanted Billy White, her husband, to die the coming Monday night.

She promised Taylor that she would give him a down

payment. Her husband's new Chevy Lumina van, and then when his insurance paid up, she would pay the remainder of what she'd promised. Twenty-thousand dollars.

The wheels were in motion.

* * *

At forty years of age, Ernest Basden still lived with his oldest sister, Rose. Rose was James Lynwood Taylor's *mother*. Ernest was the youngest of ten children. Born and raised in Jones County, Ernest's father was sixty-three when he was born. His mother was forty-four. At the age of fourteen Ernest's mother was killed in a tragic car accident. He was left alone to be raised by his seventy-seven-year-old father.

His father was a tobacco farmer as were many in the area at the time. Being that Ernest was the youngest and the most able-bodied, he did most of the work on the farm for his elderly father. Since his mother's death his father had started to drink heavily. His father's behavior changed. He was no longer the man or the father Ernest knew him to be. He was sad all of the time.

When Ernest graduated from high school he found a summer job working at a service station in Kinston. Not long after he began working, the owner sold out and Ernest was suddenly out of a job.

One of his older brothers worked as a fork lift operator for a construction company in Wilmington, North Carolina. Ernest traveled to the coastal town and was given a job too. Working alongside his brother he was content. However, as luck would have it Ernest had been working with the construction company barely a month when a young man walked into the side of his fork life. The young man died on the way to the hospital. This was only the beginning of Ernest

Basden's trail of tragedies.

Ernest moved back to Kinston and started his own auto repair shop. He didn't seem unhappy to those who came in contact with him at the repair shop, yet family members and those that knew him well claimed he was very unhappy with his life. Many said that he drank and used drugs daily.

Maybe it was the unhappiness or the need for money to support his drug habit, but whatever his reason, Ernest had agreed to kill a man for money.

His nephew, James Lynwood Taylor was making all the arrangements with the wife of the man he was to murder. He was to act as the shooter. Nothing more. No one would be the wiser and he would be a little bit richer. It seemed like a good plan.

Ernest rehashed the plot Lynwood had discussed with him. Apparently Mrs. White had planned her husband's death in elaborate detail to Lynwood. All Ernest had to do was follow directions. He could do that. He'd been doing it most of his life. However, this time there was something to gain. Something he was in desperate need of.

Money.

All he had to do was pull the trigger and walk away. Actually, Ernest thought it was going to be the easiest money he'd ever earned. He recalled his earlier conversation with his nephew. Lynwood told him he was going to pretend to be a man by the name of Tim Conners. Mrs. White had told him her husband was very greedy and he would do just about anything in order to sell an insurance policy. She told Lynwood she would tell her husband about "Tin Conners," a wealthy landowner in Trenton. Lynwood would then pose as Tim Conners and lure Mr. White away from his vehicle. Ernest would take it from there. They were supposed to make it appear as though Billy White had been robbed. Yes, Ernest thought, it seemed simple enough. He could do this.

Saturday, January 20, 1992. Their first rehearsal. Ernest and Lynwood had planned a practice run in order to prepare for Monday night. They knew things would go off without a hitch if they took extra pains to do the job just right. They would cover their tracks, Lynwood had told him. Ernest asked about a weapon. Again, his nephew assured him that wouldn't be a problem. He would locate a pistol or a shotgun in time for Monday night.

* * *

Life was different in Jones County. Ernest knew this because he had spent most of his life in the backwater town. Once one crossed the Lenoir County line over into Jones County, it was almost like stepping into Orson Wells' infamous time machine.

It may come as a surprise to those who are not life-long residents of Jones County, but in the mid 1800's Jones County was one of the wealthiest in the nation. The wealth was chiefly in land and slavery.

Many changes occurred during the Civil War. A new system was developed around the tenant farmers and cotton began a steady decline. Jones County was the center of a war zone for Southern troops stationed in Kinston and Northern troops stationed in New Bern. When visiting Jones County it is obvious that the county has yet to completely recover. The atmosphere of the new millennium was like that of the 1950's, minus the cheerful family lives portrayed in many of the popular televisions programs that entertained many families during that time period.

While visiting Trenton, I was reminded of the once popular television program, *Mayberry*. Yet beneath the laid back southern hospitality, the town appeared tainted. The slow-pace and lack of growth might appear charming to someone coming from a large city, but to those that knew the area, knew it was also slow in many areas. Law enforcement being one of them.

* * *

CHAPTER FIFTEEN

Stay with me, God.
The night is dark, my little spark of courage dies.
The night is long; Be with me, God and make me strong.

Billy Carlyle White might have had more on his mind than business when he stopped at King's Restaurant for dinner that cold Monday night in January. Before going to the restaurant, he'd stopped by the Sheraton Hotel to see his wife who was there attending a cosmetics seminar. He had to meet a client and wanted her to know he would be later than normal getting home that night. He was always prompt and didn't want her to worry.

Before leaving the Sheraton, he gave her a final kiss goodbye, then headed for a bite to eat before driving over to Jones County. He wasn't too thrilled about going out this late, but business was business and he knew there were things one often had to do in order to stay in business. Tonight was one of those nights he was doing "what he had to do."

In 1936 Frank King built a country store, *King's*. This store would become the now popular King's BBQ Restaurant known throughout Eastern North Carolina. Its first restaurant started out in Kinston and throughout the years remained the busiest. In keeping up with the times, *King's* ships the famous barbeque anywhere in the continental United States. Billy

White often dined at King's, so the King family did not find it unusual to serve Billy White a late dinner.

Upon entering the famed establishment, Billy located a single booth toward the front of the restaurant and might have ordered a plate of barbeque. After he finished his meal, he paid for his dinner, then went to the pay phone and placed a call. He was running a bit behind and didn't want to miss out on meeting his perspective client.

It was dark and chilly that January night as Billy made his way to Jones County. He had never liked the dark, but he was sure this transaction wouldn't take that long. Then he could go home and enjoy the warmth and comfort of his dream house.

Billy White made the turn onto the logging road right where Sylvia told him. Hundreds of trees lined the old road. They were so thick Billy could barely see beyond them. He drove as far as instructed, then turned off the engine. Before he could step out of the van Billy saw a man step onto the road.

Tim Conners.

Billy wanted this over as quickly as possible. He hoped this was worth the drive and aggravation because right at that point the place gave him the creeps.

* * *

CHAPTER SIXTEEN

You may charge me with
murder-or want of sense-
(We are all of us weak at times):
But the slightest approach to a
false pretense
was never among my crimes!

Taking a set of blue prints he'd kept from a former construction company he used to work for, James Lynwood Taylor got out of his vehicle and spread the blueprints on top of the hood of the car. He was into the role. If was he to act like a wealthy landowner and builder, he was going to look the part, even if it was just him and his uncle there to watch the performance.

Ernest's role was greater than his. Taylor figured he would be the main star if this were a real performance because he was the shooter. He would do the final deed. Taylor didn't like to think too much about what he and his uncle were about to do. His solace was knowing that he could ease his conscience if he thought too much because he was not the actual killer. He was the director/producer so to speak. The stars were Ernest and Mr. White. The words coward and greed came to mind but he pushed the thought aside. He looked at his watch and saw that it was time for Mr. White to make an appearance. What would they do if he didn't show? He couldn't imagine planning it all over again. Mrs. White had never discussed that with him because it had always been assumed that Mr. White would show up and that would be the end of it. And him, he thought. Still, Taylor cringed at the thought. However, it was too late now. They were here in Jones County at the logging road Mrs. White had located. He'd already been paid fifteen-hundred dollars as a down payment, of which three-hundred he'd given to his uncle. After the murder, he would collect a hefty twenty-thousand dollars as soon as Mr. White's life insurance policy paid, not to mention that Mrs. White had promised him he could keep Mr. White's new Chevy Lumina van.

They could do this. He knew it. Mrs. White had assured him they would get away with it. If something were to happen, if they were caught . . . well, they hadn't discussed that, either. But he was positive Mrs. White knew what she was doing. He even guessed the reason she'd had them drive across the county line was because she knew the law in Jones County was . . . well, it was easy. If it came down to their getting caught, he trusted Mrs. White to advise him what he should do, after all, she'd murdered her step son almost twenty years ago and gotten away with it.

"Think he'll show?" Ernest asked as he placed the shotgun on the ground next to the right front fender of Lynwood's car. If Mr. White were to make it this far, Ernest figured with the shotgun hidden under the vehicle he wouldn't see anything that would arouse his suspicions. Yes, Ernest thought, this was smart thinking on his part.

Taylor replied, "Yeah. His wife says he'd do just about anything to sell an insurance policy."

"Well, it's gettin' late. If he don't show up soon, he might not be as greedy as his wife thinks." Ernest retorted.

"Jus' shut up! He'll be here. You're makin' me nervous." Lynwood spat back at his uncle. He looked at his watch,. They were almost thirty minutes behind schedule. Lynwood was hoping that wasn't a bad omen when he heard the crunch of tires as they rolled over the dirt road, crushing small pebbles and branches that littered the old logging road.

Rehearsal was over, Lynwood thought. Now it was time for the real thing.

Billy White got out of his van and walked toward the man who must be Tim Conners.

"Evening," Billy said.

Lynwood called out to the man. "Give me a minute. I gotta take a leak."

This was Ernest's signal. Taylor walked away from the vehicle disappearing into the darkness provided by hundreds of trees. One could only imagine what his thoughts were at that time. Did he stop and think he could prevent a man's death with a shout?

Without hesitating Ernest grabbed the shotgun, raced to the front of the car, walked up to Mr. White and pulled the trigger. The big man went down, a look of shock grazing his handsome face. Ernest popped the shell out and fired again. Nothing.

"Damn!"

The shell was stuck. He cocked the shotgun and fired a second time. This time the shotgun shell slammed into Billy White's stomach at close range.

He was down.

Taylor came out from the cover of the trees. "Man,

what the hell!"

Ernest shouted, "C'mon, let's get this over with and get outta here!"

They raced back to Lynwood's, then returned to the scene of the crime in Lynwood's Camaro. They were supposed to make this look like a robbery. Lynwood reached inside Billy White's pockets and pulled them out as though someone had rifled through them. He found a pen, a silver plated cross and some coins. He took a pocket knife and a pair of eyeglasses and tossed them above the dead man's head. There was also a key. He tossed that aside too. He felt around and found Mr. White's wallet. He took that and crammed it into his pocket. He'd have to get rid of it later, but for now he'd hang onto it. He took the dead man's ring and removed his wrist watch. Ernest stuffed them in his back pockets. He'd scope out the contents later.

"Hurry it up!" Taylor shouted to his uncle.

Neither Ernest or Taylor could look at the dead man. Once the shots had been fired, Billy's white dress shirt bled crimson and the last breath of life left his body. It might have been a few seconds, maybe even as long as a minute. Hopefully Billy White died instantly, if one can justify hoping for death. Ernest Basden figured the man couldn't have suffered much, especially after that second shot. However there was something that would haunt Ernest for the rest of his days: The look of horror on Billy White's face as he realized he was about to die.

* * *

CHAPTER SEVENTEEN

I had a pleasant time with my mind, for it was happy.

June 1967

Jeff Taylor was excited that his mother was allowing him to go on the camping trip with the Boy Scouts this weekend. He'd miss his younger half brothers, Tony and Todd, but his step dad, Leslie Ipock was home for the weekend from his job as a truck driver for Overnight Transport and would be there to take care of them. Jeff knew his brothers would be in good hands while his mother worked the night shift at Blendspun, a local company that manufactured fibers and yarn.

Jeff felt bad about leaving his little brothers at home, but he was happy about the trip. He was sure when he'd asked his mother about the camping trip, she'd say no, but it seemed as though she was as excited about his trip as he was. It was almost like she *wanted* him to go. This was unusual behavior for her. Jeff didn't always have good thoughts about his mother. Yes, he loved her, but there was a part of him that didn't like her. She wasn't like some of his friends' mothers, even though she cooked, and they always had an immaculate house, clean clothes and all the things that were essential to their day to day existence. Simply put; something was missing. He didn't always understand his mother, and at thirteen, he wasn't about to try. He loved her, yet a shadow of apprehension still lingered in the back of his mind from his younger years. He sometimes thought about that shadow at night when all was quiet, but when the shadow lifted as the beginning of a new day filtered through the window, in those hours just before dawn, he tried to put the darkness of his early childhood behind him.

But there were times when putting the past behind him wasn't quite so easy. Memories of his many childhood "accidents" could not be stopped. One memory that would stay with him for many years to come and remain quite vivid despite a future brain injury was of his mother and the "iron incident" as he'd called it. He couldn't have been more than two-years-old, but his recollection was still very clear. The iron was stainless steel, with a cloth-like cord. One end of the cord plugged into the wall, while the other end had to be plugged into the base of the iron itself. He remembered the charge of electricity that surged through him as his mother forced the part of the cord that should have been plugged into the iron down his throat. The opposite end of the cord was still plugged into the wall outlet. There'd been a trip to the emergency room. His father hadn't bothered to come to the house when his mother called about his "accident," because it seemed there were so many, and after a time, his dad knew that most of the calls were false alarms.

Jeff couldn't remember where he'd gleaned this information from; maybe an Ipock family member, but the fact remained the same. When he'd been barely a toddler, his mother had taken the cord to the iron and shoved it down his throat. His lip still displayed the scar where he'd been burned. Someone later told him, possibly his father, that it was a miracle he had a top lip left.

Another memory that had plagued him for a long time and he wasn't sure if it was a product of his imagination or if it really happened and he'd simply tried to convince himself it hadn't happened at all. Quite possibly he'd overheard his father talking about it. He hoped it was his imagination, but past experience led him to believe this memory was as real as the "iron incident." Again, he surmised that he would have been around two-years-old, give or take a few months. Possibly the cage he was placed in belonged to a family pet, although he couldn't remember having a dog, or an animal large enough to require such a big cage, but with this particular memory, the smell of feces and urine always overwhelmed him. He couldn't say how long his mother had kept him "caged" or why, but it was long enough that he'd had more than a few bowel movements, and long enough for the memory to be forever ingrained in the depths of his subconscious. Those were only a few of the memories the passage of time did not have the power to erase. For now, he was looking forward to going to Myrtle Beach, South Carolina to camp out with friends from his scout troop.

* * *

CHAPTER EIGHTEEN

You may fool all the people some of the time; you can even fool some of the people all the time; but you can't fool all of the people all of the time.

Bud and Dorothy Harris, residents of Kinston and friends of the Ipock family were out for the evening with time on their hands. They agreed they needed to pay Leslie and Sylvia Ipock a long overdue visit, but as chance would have it, they learned that Sylvia was working that evening and wouldn't return until late that night.

Dorothy was good friends with Sylvia and Leslie, but saw no point in going for a visit with just Leslie and the two youngest boys. Besides, Leslie hadn't been feeling well, according to Sylvia. She'd told Dorothy that the chemicals Leslie was hauling were poisonous, making him ill. Dorothy didn't want to intrude if that were the case. There would be other times. Little did Dorothy Harris know what she might have seen, or at least postponed, had she made a visit to the Ipock household that summer evening in 1967.

Dorothy and Sylvia had shared mutual interests for many years. They attended the same church, participated in church functions together. Both were upstanding women in their communities. Sylvia was always quick to do a good need for those in need as was Dorothy Harris.

When Dorothy learned the next morning that Leslie Ipock was dead, she was stunned. He was a young man, with no apparent illness. Dorothy recalled Sylvia had once mentioned he'd had trouble when breathing in the presence of the chemicals that he hauled for Overnight Transport, but Sylvia assured her it was nothing more than "part of the job" and that Leslie would be fine. She reminded Dorothy that Overnight trucks always had signs to let the public know they were hauling dangerous chemicals. But Dorothy knew that could not be Leslie's cause of death. There had to be more.

The next day Dorothy learned that Leslie Ipock had committed suicide.

Grief stricken and numbed by the news, Dorothy felt it was her duty to visit Sylvia as soon as she learned of the tragic news. Knowing she would be devastated, Dorothy hurried to the aid of her friend.

When she arrived, she was amazed to find Sylvia in the middle of her living room, the ironing board set up, with Sylvia contentedly ironing as though this were just an ordinary day. The two youngest boys were home, but at the time Dorothy figured they were too young to understand the tragedy that had befallen their young father.

"Sylvia, I'm so sorry." Dorothy knew the words were cliche, but what else was there to say?

"Yes, so am I." Sylvia said and continued to iron.

Dorothy saw a few tears well up in her friend's eyes, but that was it. Could it be Sylvia was in shock and this was her way of dealing with her loss? Dorothy wasn't sure what to make of her friend's lack of emotion.

Knowing it might not be the perfect time, but Dorothy figured there was never a perfect time in situations such as the one she was currently in, she proceeded to question Sylvia about Leslie's death.

"Why, Sylvia? What happened?"

Sylvia stopped ironing and looked off into the distance as though she were somewhere else, not in the living room of her small home discussing the suicide of her second husband.

"Leslie was upset with me last night."

"Why?" Dorothy asked.

"He knew I was working the late shift when I left for work. He didn't like me working nights."

"Well, it's not like he didn't know ahead of time. I sure can't see this making Leslie mad."

Sylvia glared at her. "It did. He came to Blendspun last night while I was working. He told me he wanted me to come home with him."

Dorothy thought that odd, but didn't say anything. Sylvia continued to tell her friend the story.

"I told Leslie I'd be off work at midnight. I'd be right home then." Sylvia took another article of clothing and began to iron. "I came home. Leslie was in the bedroom. I went to the room and tried the knob, but he had the door locked. I just assumed he was pouting. I left him alone, I didn't want to bother him.

"The next morning when I got up, Leslie still hadn't come out of the bedroom. I decided I'd better get the key and unlock the door. When I opened the door there was Leslie, lying on the bed. I called out to him, but there was no response. Then I knew. I walked over to the bed. There was blood everywhere. I saw the gun in his hand. And of course, you know the rest."

Shocked that her friend could recite the tales of her

current tragedy so calmly, Dorothy remained quite for a few minutes allowing Sylvia's words to sink in.

"I'm sorry, Sylvia. Is there anything I can do?"

"No, the police have made their report, a definite suicide, so I just have to make the necessary funeral arrangements. They said there wouldn't be an autopsy under the circumstances."

"You let me know if I can do anything, you hear?" Dorothy hugged her friend and left. She needed to see her husband Bud. She needed his comfort.

Dorothy told Bud of last night's events and he didn't appear surprised at all.

"Dorothy, I'd bet she killed him herself."

"Bud! I can't believe you'd say such a thing about Sylvia. She's my friend!"

"Let me just say this; I wouldn't put anything past that woman."

* * *

CHAPTER NINETEEN

When they told me yesterday
what had happened, I felt like the
moon, the stars and all the planets had fallen on me.

Leslie Ipock's brothers and sisters were shocked when they learned of their brother's suicide. Sylvia told them how depressed he'd become over his ailing health. Leslie's family members had no idea he was sick, let alone depressed and suicidal. Melba, Leslie's sister recalled a time when Leslie complained about numbness in his limbs. He was hospitalized at the time, but nothing serious was found or was in question.

Some family members swore Leslie was not the kind of man to take his own life. It went against every fiber of his being. In hindsight the family would remember Leslie's illness and wonder if someone had tried to poison him. Leslie Ipock's family simply assumed that whatever ailed him would go away and he would get on with his life.

Rumors about the investigation into Leslie's death started to swarm throughout Kinston. Upon the death of her husband Sylvia gained about two-thousand dollars worth of automobiles, a measly ten-dollars and eighty-five cents in cash, plus six-hundred-fourteen dollars worth of stock from Leslie's employer, Overnight Trucking. The amount of life insurance wasn't listed in his estate file, but Glen Falls Insurance

Company secured two-thousand-eight-hundred and fifty dollars required for Sylvia to become administratrix of her husband's estate.

All officials declared Leslie Ipock's death a suicide. Again, the rumor mill was still working at top speed. One of the most damning rumors was that Leslie Ipock had been right-handed. When police officers arrived on the scene at Roseanne Drive, they were not mistaken when they pulled the gun from Leslie's Ipock's *left* hand. More than twenty years later this rumor was confirmed to be true by a fellow police officer who investigated Mr. Ipock's death.

* * *

CHAPTER TWENTY

It was a sad, sad day.

June 21, 1973
Evening

Steven White was overwhelmed with grief. He lay on his bed in the room he'd shared with Little Bill. Reminders of him were everywhere. His toys, his bed, even his little boy scent still lingered in the room. His little brother's smiling face. Gone forever. Steven could not come to terms with the loss. It had only been a few hours ago that he'd seen Little Bill alive and well.

Steven tried to recall how his little brother acted, but nothing popped into his head. He was afraid he might forget him. It seemed so unreal that his brother would never been seen or heard again. Tears swelled in his eyes. He'd miss all of Little Bill's funny accidents, his sweet face and more than anything he would miss being a big brother to him. He smashed his face into his pillow and sobbed.

He heard voices coming from the living room. The neighbors were coming to offer their condolences to his dad and stepmother. Steven wished he could erase the past twenty-four hours, pretend they never happened. Again, he pushed his face into his pillow muffling his cries. He heard his bedroom door open and looked up, hoping to see his dad. Instead it was her.

"What's the matter with you? Stop that damn crying!"

Steven looked at his stepmother, not quite comprehending her words.

Time stopped.

Steven heard Pete Barnes and his wife Judy as they arrived. Pete drove his stepmother and Little Bill to the emergency room that day. Oh, how he wished he would've stayed home that day instead of going to the pool. Maybe he could've helped Little Bill. He'd heard his stepmother crying earlier to his grandparents, telling them she'd done everything in her power to save Little Bill. He wondered just how hard she'd tried.

"I said what's the matter with you?" His stepmother shouted in a hushed voice.

Right then he wanted to get up from his bed and knock the living hell out of her. He wanted to scream and holler at her, call her all kinds of bad names, but shock and a new and different kind of fear prevented him from saying the words.

She remained in his doorway, the light from the living room giving her features a wicked look. Like a witch. The black dress she wore was perfect, he thought. The pearls around her neck were supposed to make her look like everyone else's mom. But Steven wasn't fooled.

"Are you going to answer me or what?" She persisted.

Steven looked at his stepmother and simply said, "Little Bill. I miss him."

With that she shook her head and stated flatly, "You'll get over it. Now, we've got work to do. I want you to start packing his things. I want them out of this room. Tonight." She turned and left him staring after her.

In all of his ten years, Steven had never known anyone that was quite as mean as his stepmother.

Not even Cinderella's.

* * *

CHAPTER TWENTY ONE

A simple child
That lightly draws its breath,
And feels its life in every limb,
What should it know of death?

Devastated didn't even begin to come close to describing the emotions of the White family. The loss of Little Bill was earth shattering. Never in a million years had they thought anything like this could happen in their family. Like all families they had their share of problems, especially since their father had married Sylvia, but nothing could compare to losing Little Bill.

The few short years he'd spent in the world hadn't been pleasant, starting with his biological mother. Mental illness plagued her throughout Little Bill's infancy while Billy White tried to climb the corporate ladder and did the best he could. For many months Little Bill would be sent to spend time with Leslie and Geneva (Bonnie) White, Billy's oldest brother and sister-in-law. They begged Billy to let them adopt, but he refused saying that he wanted to keep the family together. Soon, he'd said, Little Bill would be old enough to attend Kiddy College. By then, Billy explained to his older brother, the older kids would be able to help care for him in the evenings until he returned from work. Then he'd married

Sylvia and there was no need for a babysitter. Little Bill now had a stepmother.

And now he was dead.

Leslie and Bonnie were crushed when they heard the news. It was impossible! He was barely four-years-old. He was a normal, healthy child. Upon hearing the story of how Little Bill died, it was almost too much for the couple to handle. They loved their nephew like a son. Visions of what the little tyke must have suffered through crushed the entire White family. With the news still fresh and emotions raw, Leslie and Bonnie knew it wasn't the time or place to ask the hundreds of questions that they wanted to ask.

On the evening of Little Bill's death, Leslie and Bonnie went to Billy's and Sylvia's knowing they would be needed.

Bonnie recalled hearing Sylvia tell her mother and father-in-law what had happened earlier that afternoon, crying when she told her father-in-law, "Grand daddy, I tried."

"He was playing in the breakfast room sitting under the kitchen table. I stepped out to the garage to get some string beans from the refrigerator. I came back inside and heard him making a noise. I went in and saw that he was choking on the plastic. I tried to pull it out, I could feel it with my finger, I just couldn't get a firm grip on it.

"I picked the baby up and put him in the car. Somehow I managed to get out of the drive and that's when I saw Pete. He drove us to the hospital."

This version would be the first of many in the days to come. One family member said Sylvia told her Little Bill had choked on a Corn Flakes wrapper, then in the next breath said he'd torn off the plastic that she'd used to bandage a burnt leg he'd suffered with a few weeks ago. Another family member was told he'd choked on a Lincoln Log. It would take almost twenty-years for the truth to come out.

After Little Bill's death former friends of Sylvia's began to question some of her past behavior with Little Bill.

Barbara Paderick had been friends with Sylvia for more than twenty years. She lived across the street from them in the house on Hodges Road. She remembered Little Bill as being a sweet, lovable little boy. He didn't appear to have any outwardly noticeable problems. Barbara would visit the White household three or four times a month. She often thought it strange that Sylvia rarely showed the precious toddler any kind of affection. She never hugged or kissed him or whispered funny little words in his ear.

Once she'd taken a bottle of Orange Crush over for Little Bill to have as a treat. When Sylvia saw the bottle of soda, she yanked it away saying, "It makes him hyper. He can't have it."

Another time Barbara brought over a coloring book and a box of Crayons. Sylvia was not pleased by the gift. Sylvia gave Little Bill the coloring book but refused to give him the box of Crayons for fear he might make a mark on her clean walls.

As people tend to do when such a terrible tragedy takes place, memories resurface and they wonder why they didn't acknowledge what was staring them right in their face.

Barbara recalled a couple of times about three to four weeks before Little Bill died. She'd been to Sylvia's and saw that Little Bill's leg was covered in bandages. Gauze covered him from the hip down on his right leg. A week or so later Barbara saw the bandages were still on his leg, but this time they were covered with plastic wrap. Unable to hold back her curiosity, Barbara questioned Sylvia about Little Bill's accident.

Sylvia explained. "Oh, well Billy came home for lunch that day and told me not to cook anything for dinner. He wanted to grill out. I put Little Bill down for his nap. He must have sneaked out the front door while I was busy in the kitchen."

Barbara thought it strange that Little Bill would use the front door since the family almost always used the back door. She thought the front door would be too heavy for a four-year-old to open.

Sylvia continued with her story. "He went outside and found the gas can that had been run over by one of the older children. I was preparing some vegetables and I looked out and saw smoke. He'd set his clothes on fire. I ran outside and rolled him around on the ground, but he was still on fire. I got the hose that one of the boys had left on and was able to spray him and put out the fire."

A few days later Barbara returned to the White home. Sylvia was talking to Dr. Payne Dale on the phone. She held a handful of plastic in her hand, then placed her other hand over the mouthpiece of the phone so she wouldn't be overheard by someone in the doctor's office. She spoke to Little Bill. "Dr. Dale is going to be very upset with you for tearing that bandage off."

After Little Bill died Barbara recalled a comment Sylvia made two to three weeks prior to the toddler's death. Sylvia told Barbara Little Bill had started tearing the plastic off his leg and chewing it.

Was this an omen or was Sylvia setting up the scene

for her plans with Little Bill?

And yet there was another story Sylvia told her friend about the events leading up to Little Bill's death.

"Sylvia told me she ran over to my house and I was not home. From there she went to the swimming pool thinking the lifeguard would be on duty and would help her. Then she said she saw a man on Hodges Road and he drove her to the hospital. The baby was already dead when he picked her up."

More and more versions of the child's death were shared with family and friends.

Sylvia told this one herself to the White family. "I'd been to the cleaners. When I came inside I placed the dry cleaning bag on the sofa in the front room. I had to run out to the garage for a minute. When I came inside I walked through the front room again. I saw something on the floor that needed to be vacuumed. I got the vacuum cleaner out, ran it across the floor a few times, that's when I noticed the dry cleaning bag. I ran into the kitchen and saw that Little Bill was choking. I was terrified. I tried to remove the plastic but it wouldn't come out. I knew he needed a doctor so I drove to . . . I saw Pete Barnes, honked on the horn, he got in the car and drove to the hospital." Not a tear was shed as she recited events leading up to Little Bill's death.

Bonnie couldn't help remembering the time not too many weeks before when she and Leslie had Little Bill over. She'd given him a glass of milk. As little ones that age are wont to do, Little Bill knocked his glass of milk over. The child turned as white as the milky liquid that flowed across the table. "Please," he cried out, "Don't tell my mommy."

Bonnie's long time suspicions were about to surface.

What was even more odd, family members later

learned that just six days before Little Bill's death, Sylvia had been named co-beneficiary of a fifteen-thousand dollar life insurance policy. Sylvia made the first withdrawal December 17, 1973 in the amount of one-thousand dollars. Another was made on January 29, 1974 for one-thousand dollars; one on June 10, 1974 in the same amount; another on April 9, 1975 in the amount of five-hundred dollars; another on June 9, 1975 for five-hundred dollars; April 29, 1976 for five-hundred dollars; January 11, 1978 for five-hundred dollars and on April 6, 1978 the balance of the proceeds of twenty-five-hundred dollars was mailed to Sylvia. She received eight checks for the interest that accrued on each of the payments totaling just at three-hundred dollars.

For the White boys life got worse after Little Bill's death. It was almost as if his death had released an even deeper evil from within their stepmother. Teresa, nineteen and on her own was fortunate that she didn't live at home. Her brothers often thought how lucky she was. Sylvia made the lives of the two young White boys a living hell whenever the mood struck her.

The cruelty didn't stop as the boys aged. Steven recalled a time when he was at a local park playing with friends. One of his buddies asked to borrow his car to go to a convenient store to pick up some beer. Sylvia just so happened to be out at the same time. She passed Steven's car and thought he was driving. He was supposed to drive to the park and home. When Steven arrived home later, Sylvia confronted him. He explained to his stepmother that he'd loaned his car to a friend so he could go to the store. She refused to believe him. She repeatedly called him a liar. This went on for several minutes, her accusations, his denial. In a fit of frustration and anger Steven slapped his stepmother.

"She slumped to the floor like a puddle of Jell-O." Steven said.

His father arrived home from work immediately after this incident took place. Billy White insisted Steven apologize to his stepmother or he would have to leave. Knowing he was telling the truth, Steven refused to budge from his position. While still in high school, rather than live at home with a stepmother he would later compare to a female version of noted serial killer Ted Bundy, Steven White left the family home before he was of legal age.

With so many tragedies in his young life Steven resorted to drugs. He felt responsible for his mother's institutionalzation thanks to the horrid lies Sylvia had told him. He'd lost his little brother and in a sense, he'd lost his father. One could almost understand why Steven had chosen that path to follow at that time.

* * *

CHAPTER TWENTY TWO

Ne'er look for the birds of this
year in the nests of the last.

Years later when all of the children went away to college, shared apartments and started adult lives of their own, Billy's and Sylvia's marriage started to fall apart. Bill began drinking heavily. Sylvia was not happy about it at all. They had a social standing in Kinston now and she was not about to let a drunkard ruin her reputation. They fought often.

Once before the children were all on their own Sylvia did what would become a habit for her; she threatened to leave her husband. Billy was so upset by this that he ran outside crawled and beneath her car, telling her if she left him, it would kill him. Later this might be considered ironic.

Ever aware of her social position in Kinston, Sylvia joined the Eastern Star, the largest fraternal organization in the world. The purposes of the organization are charitable, educational, fraternal and scientific. However there is more to the organization. Dr. Rob Morris, the Poet Laureate of Masonry founded the Order using beautiful and inspiring biblical examples of heroic conduct and moral values. These portray the noble principles which should adorn the personal lives of Eastern Star members. Eastern Star strives to take good people and through uplifting and elevating associations of love and service, through precept and example build an Order which is truly dedicated to charity, truth and loving kindness. Even more ironic given Sylvia's character.

In spite of all the arguing between the couple, they never spoke of divorce. They continued to go about their daily lives as though nothing was wrong. They attended Sunday School classes together on a regular basis. For a while it seemed they were trying to put their marriage back together. When Billy admitted he had a drinking problem, instead of going the traditional route, AA or a rehabilitation center, he went to his good friend Bob Deaver for help. When Tony, Sylvia's married son and his wife began to have martial problems, Tony asked for Billy's help. He sought out Bob Deaver to advise the young couple.

Billy was very devoted to Sylvia and would do whatever it took to see her happiness. Rachel Thompson and her husband A.C. sat next to the Whites in Sunday School.

One particular Sunday, Rachel remembered Sylvia shouting out to no one in particular, "Well, I for one can't understand why people who live the good life can't seem to get anywhere." Billy nudged Sylvia and Rachel could tell he was embarrassed by his wife's words. She figured there must be an underlying meaning to her words. A meaning that only she and Billy were privy to.

After class that Sunday all of the parishioners were given a silver-plated cross. Billy took comfort in the small object and started carrying it in his pocket all the time. Little did Billy White know this would later become evidence.

* * *

CHAPTER TWENTY THREE

Nursing her wrath to keep it warm.

Wanting more in her life besides cooking, cleaning and trying keep Billy sober, Sylvia applied and got the position as a house parent at The Caswell Center in Kinston, a state funded home for the mentally retarded.

Many of Kinston's residents resented Sylvia's position at Caswell Center. Some felt she was taking jobs from those who really needed to work. Over the years Billy White had made large sums of money, gaining him the financial success that he worked so hard to achieve. His wife didn't *have* to work. Billy was an active participant in the GOP party, a contributor as well as a supporter. Those "in the know" in Kinston believe it was through Billy's connections with Governor Hunt and Harold Hardison that allowed Sylvia to hold the job that so many others desperately needed. According to her supervisor *Jane Reynolds, when Sylvia applied for the job she was labeled a "political-must-hire."

When first interviewed for the position, Sylvia was asked why she wanted this job. A lot of her friends and family members thought it odd that she would take such a low paying job, but when forced to give an answer she explained, "This is a way I can give back to help people in need."

Many of Sylvia's co-workers found her difficult and

hard to get along with. At times, some said she was down right mean. One instance that Jane Reynolds recalled bears repeating.

"Sylvia challenged everyone and everything. She always thought she knew more than the rest of us. At the time, I remember thinking she was about the meanest woman I'd ever met. However, she was a good worker and did an excellent job. She just couldn't get along well with others. She was a snob and thought she was better than the rest of her co-workers.

"At Caswell, our unit worked with the mentally retarded geriatric patients ages sixty-five and up. We were accredited by the State of North Carolina and also by the federal government. We had very high standards for our guests and our employees. We cared about our patients and it was our duty to help them learn as much as possible.

"If ever there was a complaint filed for any reason, it had to be investigated by the proper federal officials. Sylvia was hired as a health care tech, a nurses aid. There were certain aspects to the job that anyone would find challenging. Bed pans and bathroom habits weren't on top of anyone's list of favorite duties. Apparently Sylvia decided this was part of her job that she shouldn't have to do.

"She made a complaint to Governor Hunt's office that shocked the entire unit. The first one that stands out is the time she accused the day shift employees of giving the residents too many enemas. Sylvia said, 'We're cleaning up way too much shit on the night shift.' Of course that had to be investigated by the Governor's office. After an investigation her claims were found to be unsubstantiated."

"This still did not stop Sylvia from calling the

Governor's hotline. Another complaint I'll never forget was the time she called the Governor's office and told the proper officials we were forcing the residents out of bed and making them come to the dinner table naked.

"Again this wasn't substantiated. The complaints kept coming. All of us knew where they were coming from. We kept quiet and went about our jobs.

"Being Sylvia's direct supervisor it was up to me to give her an evaluation. In order to receive a raise, you had to show improvement in your work performance. If you received "all good" you were off probation. When I did Sylvia's evaluation, she received "all good" on everything. To most this would have been a satisfactory report. Not so according to Mrs. White.

"After receiving her evaluation she was mad."

"This is the worst evaluation I've ever seen." Sylvia shouted to Jane.

Jane was shocked at Sylvia's wild behavior. "That's a good evaluation Sylvia."

Sylvia continued to blast Jane out.

"Her face was red, her arms were gesturing wildly. I thought for a minute she was going to hit me."

"I don't have to take your shit. Don't have to, not going to." Sylvia continued shouting to Jane.

"That's your prerogative." Jane said as calmly as she could.

Sylvia stormed out of the room only to return twenty minutes later. Jane was frightened and for a moment wondered if Sylvia had left her office, only to return with a weapon. Apparently Sylvia had spoken with the central supervisors on each shift, thinking possibly they would agree that she deserved a much better evaluation.

Startled at the sudden interruption, Jane stood her ground with the wild woman. "Get control of yourself."

Sylvia waved the report around hollering. "I'm not gonna take this crap!"

"Leave this office at once before I call security!" Jane stated firmly to the wild employee in front of her desk.

With those last words, Sylvia left her office. Jane was beyond relieved.

That evening when Jane told her husband about the incident she recalled saying, "For the first time ever an employee put me in harm's way."

"Be very careful," her husband told her. Eventually their unit received so many complaints that it was dismantled. Years later Jane would recall Sylvia White's behavior and label her with a personality disorder and anti-social behavior.

* * *

Little Bill's grave, next to his father's, Billy White Sr.

This will be Sylvia Ipock-White's final resting place. This grave site is next to Leslie Ipock's, her second husband, whose 1967 suicide still remains under suspicion.

Billy White's home on Roseanne Drive. This is where he lived when he began to date Sylvia Ipock.

Sylvia Ipock's home on Roseanne Drive. She lived on the same street as Billy White. This is the house where Leslie Ipock was said to have committed suicide.

The White home on Hodges Road, the house where Little Bill died.

The newly constructed dream home where Billy White lived before his murder in 1992.

Lenoir Memorial Hospital's Emergency room. The door Sylvia rushed through carrying Little Bill.

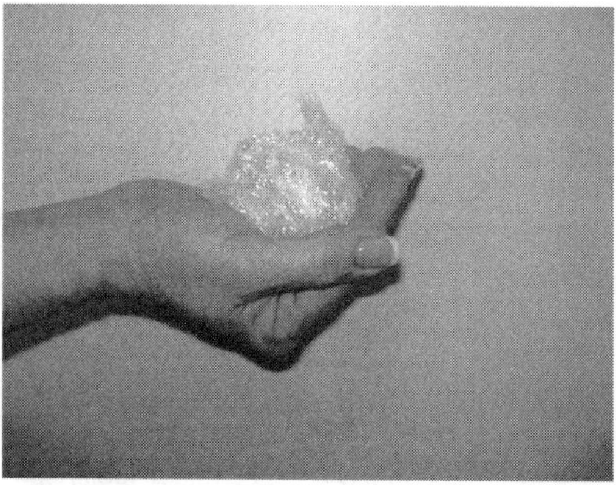

A replica of the plastic Dr. Sabiston removed from Little Bill's throat.

King's Restaurant where Billy White had dinner the night of his murder.

The booth where Billy White sat as he ate his last meal.

The old logging road in Jones County where Billy White's bloodied body was found.

The Jones County Courthouse and Sheriff's Department in Trenton, North Carolina.

The staircase leading downstairs to the jail cells where Lynwood, Ernest and Sylvia were taken after their arrest.

The Jones County Courthouse hallway where Sylvia roamed freely during her incarceration.

Sylvia Ipock White

James Lynwood Taylor

Ernest Wesley Basden

Bennett Simms, Detective with the Lenoir County Sheriff's Department. He was instrumental in reopening the investigation of Little Bill's death.

Teresa White-Murray, Steven White, Dan White and Georgia White (Billy White's mother).

Susan Manning, the nurse who held the plastic that was removed from Little Bill's throat, with Suzanne Barr.

6381

North Carolina State Board of Health
OFFICE OF THE CHIEF MEDICAL EXAMINER
CHAPEL HILL, NORTH CAROLINA 27514

SEP 10 1973

☑ Resident
☐ Nonresident

REPORT OF INVESTIGATION BY MEDICAL EXAMINER

DECEDENT Billy C. White II (First name / Middle name / Last name) AGE 4 SEX Male RACE White

ADDRESS 2800 Hodges Rd. Kinston, N. C. (Number and Street / City / County) M W S D OCCUPATION: child

TYPE OF DEATH: (Check one only)
Sudden in apparent health ☐
Unattended by a physician ☐
In police custody ☐

Violent or Unnatural ☒ plastic
Suspicious ☐ Means: (Agency or Obje
Unusual ☐
Operating Room or Operative Death ☐

	LAST SEEN ALIVE	INJURY OR ILLNESS	DEATH	MEDICAL EXAMINER NOTIFIED	VIEW OF BODY	POLICE NOTIFIED	IF MOTOR VEHICLE ACCIDENT CHECK ONE OF THE FOLLOWING
DATE	6-21-73	6-21-73	6-21-73	6-21-73	6-21-73		DRIVER ☐ PASSENGER ☐
TIME	3:30 p.m.				3:30 P.m.		PEDESTRIAN ☐

M.E. NOTIFIED BY: Lenoir Memorial Hospital ADDRESS Kinston, N. C.

	LOCATION	COUNTY	TYPE OF PREMISES (E. G., HOSPITAL, HOTEL, HIGHWAY, ETC.)
INJURY OR ONSET OF ILLNESS	Home-2800 Hodges Rd.	Lenoir	HOme
DEATH	Home	Lenoir	Home
VIEWING OF BODY BY MEDICAL EXAMINER	Lenoir Memorial Hosp	Lenoir	Hospital

DESCRIPTION OF BODY		NOSE	MOUTH	EARS	NON FATAL WOUNDS	RIGOR	LIVOR
CLOTHED ☒ UNCLOTHED ☐	BLOOD				ABRASION ☐ BURN ☐	JAW ☐ ARMS ☐	ANTERIOR ☐
PARTLY CLOTHED ☐ HAIR	FROTH				CONTUSION ☐ STAB ☐	NECK ☐ CHEST ☐	POSTERIOR ☐
BEARD ___ MUSTACHE ___	OTHER (Sand, dirt, water, etc.)				GUNSHOT ☐ INCISED ☐	BACK ☐ ABDOMEN ☐	LATERAL ☐
CIRCUMCISED ☐ PUPILS: R ___ L ___					LACERATION ☐	LEGS ☐	REGIONAL ___
EYES: Color ___ OPACITIES, ETC.	WEIGHT ___ LENGTH ___				FRACTURE ☐ DISTRIBUTION: SCALP ☐ FACE ☐ NECK ☐ CHEST ☐ BACK ☐ ABDOMEN ☐ ARMS ☐ LEGS ☐		
	BODY HEAT:						

FATAL WOUNDS

TYPE (GUNSHOT, INCISED, STAB, ETC.)	SIZE	SHAPE	LOCATION	PLANE, LINE OR DIRECTION
0	E911			

Probable cause of death:
asphyxiation due to tracheal foreign body

Manner of death: (*Check one only*)
~~Accident~~ ☒ Suicide ☐ Homicide ☒
Natural ☐ Unknown ☐ Pending ☐

ME Autopsy Authorized: Yes ☐ No ☒
Non-ME Autopsy Done: Yes ☐ No ☐
Pathologist ___

I hereby certify that after receiving notice of the death described herein I took charge of the body and made inquiries regarding the cause of death in accordance with Art. 21, Chapter 130 of the General Statutes of North Carolina and the information contained herein regarding such death is true and correct to the best of my knowledge and belief.

9-4-73 — Date
Lenoir — County of Appointment
Frank Sabiston, Jr., M.D. — Signature of Medical Examiner

Form 1
SBH Form 1114 Rev. 2/70
Medical Examiner

CHIEF MEDICAL EXAMINER 5408

Little Bill's amended Report of Investigation By Medical Examiner, dated September 4, 1973, almost three months after his death.

CHAPTER TWENTY FOUR

It is acknowledged that neither convict prisons, nor the hulks, nor any system of hard labour ever cured a criminal.

Ernest Basden knew the minute he asked to speak with the police there was no turning back. He sighed, knowing he was about to do the right thing, sorry that he'd done it in the first place. He should've listened to his gut. He should've gone to the police himself when Mrs. White approached Taylor. He should have done a lot of things, but it was too late for recriminations now.

Eric Wayne Smith, special agent for the North Carolina State Bureau of Investigation had worked in the Jacksonville, North Carolina district for more than six years. His duties were to assist local law enforcement agencies in criminal investigations upon request. The majority of his experience was investigating homicides.

"You wanted to see me?" Smith asked.

Taylor was already in jail and Basden figured it wouldn't take too long before he told the cops about his role in Mr. White's death and he would be in jail right alongside his cousin. It would look better if he simply confessed and got it over with. He didn't have much of a life as it was. Spending what remained of it behind bars would almost be a relief.

"Yeah," Ernest stated flatly.

Ernest Basden told this horrific story to his court-appointed attorney, William E. Craft.

"I was livin' with my oldest sister, Lynwood's mother at the time. I was workin' as a mechanic. Lynwood would stop by the shop sometimes and we'd talk. It was in the summer of 1991 Lynwood had come by my shop one day and said he had this girl that wanted him to kill her husband. I told him he was crazy. I just passed it off. There wasn't a whole lot more said about it." Ernest took a deep breath.

"Did you see him and discuss this at another time?"

"He mentioned it again, two to three months later, something like that," Ernest said.

"Exactly how did he mention it? Did he come by your shop again?"

"Well, every time it was talked about, he came to my shop during the day when I was workin'. He brought it up again . . . that this lady was tryin' to, you know, kept callin' him, trying to get him to kill her husband."

"Did he go into any details at that time about who the lady was?"

"No."

"Did he give any details about how long he knew this lady?"

Again, Ernest answered, "No."

"Did he ever come by your shop anymore to discuss this matter?"

"I saw him regular, yes."

"He didn't discuss this matter at every visit, is that right?" The question was asked for clarification.

Ernest nodded. "Right. It was the 17th, 16th or 17th, the

Thursday or Friday, I think it was a Friday before and he brought it up again and he came by the shop. He brought it up again and, you know, went on and on. He told me how this woman had been trying to kill her husband through poisonous plants, had been to the library and got a book on poisonous plants."

"Did Lynwood tell you that he went to the library with her to help her one time?"

"I don't recall that."

"You don't recall that?" The questioner parroted.

"Seems like he did. I just don't recall." Ernest said.

"What else did he tell you? Did he tell you who the woman was then when he was talking about that?"

Ernest was asked to continue. "He told me he had gotten some heroin for her and I forgot how they used it. It didn't work. And the conversation just continued."

"Wait just a minute. You say he got some heroine for her? Did he say that was in an attempt to kill her husband?"

"Yes, sir."

"And you say he didn't say how he used it?"

"No, sir."

"Did he tell you that Mrs. White had tried to poison her husband before?"

"Yes, sir," Ernest said.

"And how did she try to do that? Do you remember?"

"Putting poison in his food, cooking it in his foods."

"And evidently it didn't work?"

"No," Ernest said.

"Was it after that when she asked Lynwood to get some heroin for her?"

"Yes."

"And did Lynwood say that he did do that?"

"Yes, sir."

"Did he say how they were planning to use the heroin to kill Mr. White?"

"No."

"Did he tell you about Mrs. White or what he and Mrs. White had done?"

Ernest shifted in his chair. "Well, at that point that was all, but he continued to elaborate or, you know, tell the details of how Mrs. White had told him that Mr. White had beaten her and made her do horrible things in sex and it just, you know?"

"That she wanted him dead? Is that what she told?"

"Yes, sir."

"When was it you agreed to participate in it?"

"It was later on in that conversation. I don't remember just how it was put to me or the words he used, but I agreed to."

"Did he tell you what Mrs. White had promised him to kill her husband?"

"Yes, sir. He said she was giving him twenty-thousand dollars and Mr. White's van."

"Did she state where she was going to get the money?"

"From the insurance."

"Did Lynwood state anything about how he had told her that he would kill the husband himself?"

"I think the words he used when he told me were, 'I'll take care of it.'"

"Did he tell you what plans he and Mrs. White had for the killing?"

"Yes. He told me he had come up with that name Tim Conners and that this Tim Conners was supposedly to try and buy a big insurance policy from Mr. White."

"Was Lynwood Taylor to pose as Tim Conners?"

"Yes, sir."

"What else did they plan after that? I mean, how did they plan that this would take place?"

Ernest shook his head. "Well, this Tim Conners supposedly was, I think he said from Durham and had bought some property in Jones County. He was going to build a house or develop it or whatever. Lynwood was to call him and set up a meeting with him to talk about this insurance policy."

"Well, did Lynwood tell you he did that?"

"He did, yes, well he called him that Monday evening."

"And how did Mr. White know where to go to meet him?"

"Lynwood had made, he either had made up a map or he and Mrs. White made up a map together for Mrs. White to give to Mr. White to get to the location."

"Did Lynwood tell you how many times he met with Mrs. White concerning this matter?"

"No, he didn't give me a number of times, but he told me that she kept calling him asking him about it."

"Did he always go to her house when he wanted to talk to her?"

"I really don't know."

"Did he ever tell you that he met her at any other places?"

"He never told me whether he did or didn't."

"He told you the plans they had for the killing?"

"Yes, sir. After I had agreed to do it."

"Did you have anything to do with the planning or

with the weapons?"

"No, sir. He took care of all of that. That Sunday he took me to the location and he went to several other places, but we ended up going back to the first place he went."

"What did he tell you about the gun? Did you own a gun, a shotgun or any kind of weapon?"

"No, sir. I've never owned a gun."

"What did Lynwood tell you about the weapon?"

"He was going to buy a pistol and then I don't remember if he said if it was that Sunday or the Monday evening that he said he had a shotgun that he was going to use."

"What did he tell you about the shotgun shells? Did he tell you to get the shells?"

"No, sir. He had all that too."

"How did you and him get together on the day of the killing? Did he come by and pick you up?"

"I went to his house."

"Did he leave the gun and everything in the car?"

"He put it in the car while I was there."

"Did he tell you what he wanted you to do?"

"Yes. He had a pair of tennis shoes for me to wear. Afterwards we were to come back to his house, burn our clothes and shoes, then cut the gun up and put it in cement and throw it in the river."

"Did he tell you that's what you were supposed to wear? The tennis shoes?"

"Yes, sir. It was through his suggestions, yes."

"Was there any reason on that date, , did he tell you that he had set up a time to meet with Mr. White?"

"Yes, sir. Well, he left while, I got here earlier on the

evening somewhere around 5:30 or so and he left to go call Mr. White. He left the house."

"Did he tell you that he had talked to Mr. White?"

"Yes, sir."

"Did Mr. White say anything about being a little late or anything?"

"Well, I think Lynwood suggested a time and Mr. White couldn't be there at that time or whatever and they agreed upon 8:30 as the final time."

"The day that this took place, was it good and dark at 8:30?"

"Yes, sir."

"And you rode out with Lynwood to the designated place and waited for Mr. White, is that right?"

"Yes, Sir. We rode in his wife's Oldsmobile."

"What did you do when Mr. White got there? Where were you? Were you in the car or out of the car?"

"No, we were both standing at the right front of the car. Lynwood had gotten some kind of pamphlet or whatever to lay it on the hood of the car to look like he was looking at some plans, development plans or whatever because he had told Mr. White, that you know, he was doing construction work on his property and he was meeting with a contractor."

"Where was the shotgun?"

"It was on the ground to the left of the car, the driver's side."

"Were you the one that actually shot Mr. White?"

"Yes, sir. When I shot him, he just fell to the ground."

* * *

CHAPTER TWENTY FIVE

To tell tales out of schoole

Sylvia White paced back and forth in her living room .She should have received a telephone call by now. She was sure something must have gone wrong when the phone rang. She breathed a sigh of relief before picking up the receiver.

"Hello?"

"It's done." The line went dead.

Sylvia Ipock White let out another anxious sigh of relief. Finally. It was done and over with. No more hastily planned meetings, no more begging and pleading. Her wish had been granted. She'd had to pay a price, but she knew from past experience it would be worth it in the end. She could live the life she chose without interference from anyone.

Now it was simply a waiting game. She knew what she had to do; she was familiar with the role of widow. She'd been there once before and she had managed to get through it. She was certain she could do it a second time.

Sylvia made the call that she had been dreading; the call to the police to report her husband as missing.

Next on her "widows list of things to do" was to make the necessary funeral arrangements, but first she had to continue on as if nothing were out of the ordinary. Sylvia would bide her time. She knew the good things in life didn't come as easily as some thought. She also knew that sometimes you had to give fate a little guidance. What she didn't know was that someone had received a similar phone call just seconds before she had answered her telephone. This was just another horrendous mistake in what would later become one of many.

Sylvia continued pacing back and forth in the living room. She went to her bedroom and pulled on her favorite red bath robe and returned to the living room to wait for the call she knew was inevitable. While waiting to gear the fate of her husband, she nodded off.

One cannot know what Sylvia White's thoughts were as she dozed. Maybe she dreamed of her deceased husband? Maybe she dreamt of the small fortune she was about to recieve? Maybe she dreamt of finally having her dream home all to herself. Or maybe her mind was just a total blank. Maybe all she felt was relief. For now, Sylvia White knew there was nothing to do but wait.

* * *

CHAPTER TWENTY SIX

How shall we praise the magnificent of the dead.

Word of Billy White's murder continued to spread throughout the community like wildfire. Citizens double locked their doors and looked twice at strangers Who could commit such a cruel and senseless crime? Talk and theories were rampant those first few days after Mr. White's untimely death.

After learning of Billy White's terrible fate, friends and family gathered inside the White home on Roseanne Drive to offer the grieving widow their condolences. Sylvia continued treading back and forth. She was a wreck.

"Please, this can't be happening!" Sylvia cried out.

As friends and family members prayed for Billy's White family, police officers were suddenly steered in a different direction. When they checked out the phone call they had received earlier via the local Crimestoppers, they were sure their luck was about to change.

* * *

Kinston police knew they had their man. James Lynwood Taylor was a cold-blooded killer. He'd just admitted to thc murder of Billy White. Some members of the force thought this too easy.

The first story James Lynwood Taylor told the police

was a lie. He and Ernest had agreed that if they were caught, he would take the rap. When questioned, James Lynwood Taylor did not put up a defense or say anything to indicate that he was not the trigger-man. The officers investigating the case had assumed he had shot Billy White since he hadn't said otherwise. Now, however, they mentioned the death penalty and he was getting scared. Taylor thought taking the fall for his uncle wasn't such a smart idea after all.

Taylor had been so sure they wouldn't get caught. Mrs. White had practically guaranteed it when she planned her husband's murder. Nothing was happening like she said it would. Nothing at all. Now, he couldn't believe how he'd fallen for her lies, but money does strange things to a man and he was not immune to the call of a better life.

He knew what he had to do next. He asked to speak to a police officer.

* * *

PART TWO

CHAPTER TWENTY SEVEN

But though my wing is closely bound,
My heart's at liberty;
My prison walls cannot control
The flight, the freedom of the
soul.

February 12, 1992

James Lynwood Taylor knew his days as a free man were numbered when he asked to speak to the police a second time. He was afraid in one sense and then again, he felt somewhat relieved. He didn't have what it took to carry such guilt. Maybe confessing would be good for his soul. At least he wasn't an actual murderer. He kept telling himself this over and over; then his conscience would kick in, reminding him that he was responsible for introducing the idea to his uncle. He could've told Sylvia White to go to hell. But he didn't and here he was, waiting to confess to one of the worst sins man could commit.

When the officers returned, he knew by the looks on their faces that he'd failed the polygraph. He didn't care about that. Now he simply wanted to tell the whole truth and nothing but the truth.

"So, you had something to say?" An officer asked Lynwood.

"Yeah. I want to tell you what really happened the night Mr. White died." Taylor said.

"Okay. There are a few formalities, but you just hold tight and we'll have them taken care of in no time."

The officer left the room leaving James Lynwood Taylor alone. This was it. He was doing the right thing and he knew it. Suddenly, it felt as if a burden weighing a thousand tons had been lifted from his shoulders.

Several police officers and an SBI agent returned to the room. They had a tape recorder with them along with several blank tapes. After making sure the tape recording equipment was in proper working order, Taylor was asked to tell his story, this time though, it was the truth. He told them that he was not the actual trigger-man. He said he'd been hired by Mrs. White and that Mr. White's imminent death had been in the planning stages for months. He told them he hadn't wanted to get involved with Mrs. White and her plans to kill her husband, but she'd been so persistent, he couldn't resist. He said he'd felt sorry for her. She told him her marriage was very abusive, that Billy White was weird in the sex department. He told how he'd discussed this with his uncle. He also said his uncle told Lynwood the woman was crazy. Lynwood said he knew that now, but at the time, he just wanted to do whatever he could to get her off his back.

When his uncle told him he would consider doing the job himself because he needed the money, Lynwood told Mrs. White and the plans were made. He told police that she'd given him map to the old logging road out in Jones County. She explained to him that it must look like a robbery. He agreed, telling her he knew someone who would help him kill Mr.

White. Sylvia White said she wanted it done as soon as possible. The following Monday, she'd said. She told Lynwood she planned on attending a seminar and that she would have plenty of witnesses if it were to come to that. However, she did not tell Lynwood what to do if he and his uncle were caught. He didn't think they would get caught, he told officers, because Mrs. White had gotten away with murdering her four-year old step son. He trusted that she knew what she was doing.

About a week after Mr. White's murder Lynwood went to Sylvia White's home on Eleanor Drive to collect a down payment. He told officers she had company. Her step daughter and others were there at the time. They had to be very discreet. Mrs. White gave him an envelope with fifteen-hundred dollars and said she would pay him the remainder of eighteen-thousand-five hundred as soon as her husband's insurance paid. She also reminded him that he was getting her husband's van.

Police offers asked Lynwood to call Mrs. White. He agreed and they set up a recording device to tape the phone call.

"It's me, Lynwood," he replied. "The police are questioning me. How did they get my name?"

"I haven't told the police anything," Sylvia replied.

The connection was validated for the police. Mrs. White could deny knowing Lynwood, but they had it on tape that she knew him and they were sure it was quite well. While they suspected she'd had an affair with Lynwood, he never admitted to it, but they did question a man (unidentified at the time of this writing) that told police he had been having an affair with Mrs. White. He said Mrs. White spoke to him a few weeks before her arrest. "We're not guilty of doing anything, but we have to get our stories together."

The noose was slowly tightening.

Lynwood thought if only he hadn't trusted Mrs. White. If only he hadn't been so needy and greedy. If only he'd walked away that day he went to her house to look at her windows. If he'd gone to the police then, Mr. White might still be alive and Mrs. White would be behind bars where she belonged. But "if only's" weren't going to help him now.

After making a formal statement, James Lynwood Taylor was charged with first degree murder and booked into the Jones County Jail in Trenton, North Carolina.

* * *

CHAPTER TWENTY EIGHT

All are presumed good till they are found in a fault.

February 13, 1992

Sylvia White was amazed. It had been over three weeks since Billy's murder, and she hadn't been arrested. She knew her luck would only hold out for so long. Still, she wasn't worried because they would have to prove she was involved and she knew the police would believe her over a drug informant. She smiled. Life was good.

She went about her days as the grieving widow. She might have cleaned house, ironed or planned what she would do with all the insurance money she would soon receive. What one can be sure of: Sylvia White had not planned on spending the night in jail.

At 1:15 A.M. on February 13, 1992 police officers knocked on her door at 1909 Eleanor Drive. She was startled awake when she heard the knock on her door. She grabbed her favorite bathrobe from the foot of her bed and went downstairs to answer the door.

She did not like what she saw.

Police officers greeted her at the door, then read her her Miranda rights. They explained that she was under arrest for the murder of her husband, Billy Carlyle White.

"I need to get dressed,"she told the officers.

"Ma'am, you'll have to come as you are."

Sylvia White was then taken to the Jones County jail wearing her favorite red bathrobe. Cameras from one of the local television networks were there to film her in all her glory, as well as a few newspaper reporters.

Carolyn Dunn, a reporter for Channel 12 out of New Bern, North Carolina shot out a question to Mrs. White as she was being led to the patrol car. "Mrs. White, did you kill your husband?"

Sylvia glanced around, searching for a face to go with the words. She simply stated, "I didn't have any money."

One can only wonder what Mrs. White meant when she said this to the reporter. Did she mean she 'didn't have any money' in the sense of being broke, or did she mean she 'didn't have any money' to hire a hit-man? Maybe she was simply stating her thoughts, or she just hadn't received any money from Billy White's insurance at that point. One can only speculate.

After Sylvia was formerly charged and booked into the Jones County Jail, she made her one allowed phone call to Teresa White-Murray. Teresa arrived at the jail shortly after her stepmother's phone call. The last civil words between them were Sylvia's. "I'm sorry you had to come out here so late." She gave Teresa all of her jewelry and was escorted to her cell.

* * *

CHAPTER TWENTY NINE

A liar should have a good memory

Ernest Basden might have thought that February fourteenth was nothing more than a day for sweethearts to declare their love for one another. However, if one thought of Valentine's Day in the massacre sense, then that was about to become the state of Ernest Basden's life.

After learning that his nephew James Lynwood Taylor had been arrested, followed by the arrest of Mrs. White, he knew their original plan for Lynwood to take full responsibility for Mr. White's murder would have to be squashed. He'd been to visit Lynwood, and he knew that his days as a free man were numbered. He could count the hours, possibly the minutes until he lost any control of any kind over his life. Family members had convinced him to go to the police and confess his involvement in Mr. White's death. They told him when and if this went to court it would look better for him and he might receive a lighter sentence.

The were right about certain things and dead wrong about others.

Ernest went to Jones County where he met with Eric Smith. Detective Bennet Simms with the Lenoir County Sheriff's Department was in the room as Agent Smith questioned Ernest. Both officers just happened to be in Jones County that morning to attend a hearing for Lynwood's and

Sylvia's first appearance.

Ernest gave the officers his name, age and told them that he lived with Lynwood's mother, which happened to be Ernests' sister. He explained that he almost went to the police station in Kinston, but then figured since the murder was committed in Jones County, he'd better go to the police in Trenton.

Ernest told Agent Smith and Detective Simms that whatever Lynwood had told them was the truth. He told them that he was the man responsible for shooting Billy White. Both officers stopped him at that point and advised him of his rights. He acknowledged that he understood them and signed an acknowledgment sheet. After Agent Smith was assured that Ernest understood his rights, Ernest said he would still talk even though he didn't have legal representation.

Ernest told Agent Smith that Lynwood Taylor had met a white female in the Kinston area that wanted her husband murdered. He also told Agent Smith that to his knowledge, Lynwood had met Mrs. White through an introduction from her son, Tony Ipock. Ernest related what Lynwood had told him when he was first approached by Mrs. White.

"Lynwood said he was at Mrs. White's house to fix a window. She asked him out of the blue if her could find a hit-man to kill her husband."

"Go on," Smith said.

"After a while I got myself into a financial bind. I asked Lynwood if Mrs. White's offer was still good. He told me it was."

Ernest proceeded with his story. He and Lynwood drove Lynwood's Oldsmobile over to Jones County. Once they spotted the old logging road that Mrs. White had mapped out for them, they pulled in and turned their vehicle so that it faced

State Road 1156. Then they waited.

Later they spied Billy's van as he turned onto the logging road. Mr. White for out of the van and Lynwood introduced himself as Tim Conners. He told Mr. White he had to pee. Lynwood walked over to the side of the road to pee, then Ernest explained that he then went to the driver's side of the vehicle and stooped down to the ground where they'd placed the shotgun. He told the officers he just picked the gun up and fired it at Mr. White. Ernest went on to say that he looked Mr. White.

Ernest went on to say the he looked Mr. White squarely in the eye when he pulled the trigger. Mr. White never blinked, he never flinched, he just stood there and never even tried to run. After Ernest fired the first shot, he went down. The expended shell was removed and another placed into the chamber. He fired at Mr. White a second time as he lay on the ground. He told Agent Smith that he and Lynwood left the crime scene only to return for a second time in Lynwood's Camaro because they had left the map behind that Mrs. White had given them, plus they'd forgotten to make the killing appear as though Mr. White had been robbed. Ernest said they had removed a ring from Mr. White's finger, took his wallet and a blank check.

They raced back to Lynwood's house where they both removed their clothes and burned them. They took the shotgun barrel and sawed it into three pieces with a hacksaw, then placed those three pieces in a bucket of cement. They drove over to the Oak Bridge on Highway 55 and tossed the bucket into the Neuse River. All of this for three-hundred dollars.

CHAPTER THIRTY

The search begins

Around noon on Friday February 14, 1992 SBI divers put on their gear as they prepared to search the Neuse River. It wasn't all the muddy and was much more shallow than they'd expected. They were able to stand while searching most of the area.

As a safety precaution, tow Kinston firefighters positioned themselves in a boat just under the bridge while several officials looked on from the shore.

The followed a sort of grid search pattern by combing the bottom of the river by feeling with their hands. While the current was estimated at two knots and was one of the biggest obstacles. The temperature was around fifty degrees and wasn't nearly as bad as they thought it would be.

After a few hours of searching, SBI divers found what they'd been searching for.

In a bucket that had been filled with cement, they located the three sawed-off pieces of the shotgun that was used to murder Billy White.

SBI Supervisor Bill Godley of Greenville told reporters that the divers had found "valuable evidence."

* * *

After the news of the trio's arrest, many Kinstonians

would recall instances in the past where they had encountered something that connected them with the now infamous murderess, something she said or did that now would offer some sort of explanation for her status as that of a cold-hearted killer. Even though Lynwood and Ernest were both charged with first degree murder, they were not the subject of gossip and rumors as was Sylvia White.

Gene Hawkins, who once shared office space with Billy White had this to say. "Sylvia was always cold and distant to Billy's children. Billy lost his house when they lived on Hodges Road because of his gambling debts. Sylvia never let him forget it either. Billy drew on his insurance policies and after a while, he was deemed as 'uninsurable.' Billy was a people person. Sylvia was not."

A former high school classmate, Belle remembered Sylvia. "We used to play on the girls basketball team when we both were at Grainger High. Sometimes when she would grab the ball, there would be such a look of deep anger come over her face. And she was always so pretty."

A woman who knew Sylvia when she was married to Leslie Ipock who asked not to be identified said, "There was always a dark side to Sylvia. It's a shame because her sister was so normal."

Denise Adams, Clerk of Court assistant in Jones County observed Sylvia after she was arrested and jailed in Trenton. "There was no bottom to Sylvia's eyes." Denise said she also remembered Ernst Basden because he worked her father's tobacco farm when she was in high school. "He was always nice and polite."

Jones County Deputy Clerk of Court, Sherry Jarman had a different opinion of Sylvia White. "She would always look at nothing. She was very humble."

Ronald Butts, Clerk of Court for Jones County said, "She was devoid of all emotion."

Woody Taylor, Sylvia's first husband who considers himself lucky to be alive after surviving their short marriage had this to say after learning of her arrest. "After all these years, I want to confirm that she's the same lying, conniving bitch that she always was."

There are still those that swear Sylvia is innocent. Sylvia had many opportunities to undergo a polygraph examination. Each time she was scheduled to take the exam, she was nowhere to be found. One would reason if you're innocent, given the weight of the polygraph, that would be the one appointment that you would want to show up for, come hell or high water.

* * *

CHAPTER THIRTY ONE

Nothing in excess.

The Jones County Jail in Trenton, North Carolina is not your typical twentieth-century (1992) jail. Housed downstairs in the Trenton County Courthouse, if you didn't know it was there, you would never find it. Upon entering the Courthouse, you simply made a couple of swift turns, and there it is. A deputy seated at a desk greets people as they enter the Sheriff's Department. In a hallway not more than fifty feet long directly behind the deputy's desk are the actual jail cells. The bars have been painted white many times over. The inside of the cells are what one would expect. Small, a place to sleep and idle the hours away. An inmate could easily view the comings and goings of the sheriff and his deputies.

The environment in the Jones County Jail could hardly be one that would intimidate a first-time felon, let alone three cold-blooded killers. It's a modern day version of Mayberry, minus Otis, the town drunk and Barney Fife.

The Jones County Grand jury handed down murder and conspiracy indictments against Sylvia, Lynwood and Ernest. All were being held in the Jones County Jail without bail. The trio hit thc jackpot when they landed in jail in Jones County. While each waited for their prospective trials, they were all allowed privileges that most murderers could never dream of.

Sylvia was allowed to leave her jail cell and roam the

halls of the courthouse. She could go to the soda machine and purchase a soda anytime she desired. Sometimes she was seen sitting at the front desk smoking a cigarette. She used the women's public restroom as though it were her own. Maybe this is where she would go to do her hair and make-up on those Sundays she was allowed to leave the jail to attend church. Some say she had a female chaperone when she was attending church. I would think that being allowed out of one's cell would be a huge privilege, let alone being allowed to leave the facility to attend church. It could be possible Sylvia White knew of Jones County and its lack of security. Is this why she planned her husband's murder in this county in the first place? Again, one can only speculate.

Lynwood was not treated as though he were a convicted murderer, either. Sheriff Wesley Mallard must have felt bad for him because he allowed him to leave the jail in order to work at the Sheriff's home. He was also allowed to attend meetings at Brocks Mill Pond for a motorcycle club that he belonged to. Again, this did not seem to be the type of freedom a man charged with first degree murder should have. But that was Jones County.

Ernest had freedom as well, but I was not able to ascertain exactly what type of freedom, other than he was not treated like a man charged with so serious a crime. First degree murder. He was the trigger man.

* * *

When Susan Manning learned that Sylvia White had been charged in her husband's murder, she remembered their young son who had died such a strange death twenty years ago. She had never forgotten about the beautiful little boy and had always suspected his death had not been an accident.

In 1973 nurses were not allowed to question a doctor. It was unheard of. Susan had wanted to ask Dr. Sabiston how in the world that child could have swallowed a piece of plastic so large, but she didn't. It just wasn't done. Now, however things were different. There were all kinds of agencies that checked with hospitals when a child was abused, plus doctors and nurses were better trained in identifying abuse. She felt horrible for not speaking up then, but twenty years had passed. Maybe she could voice her suspicions now.

After Sylvia's arrest Susan skimmed the paper each day. She wondered if they would address the child's death since they were reporting on Sylvia White's second husband, Leslie Ipock's death. He committed suicide, but now according to the local gossip mill, people were suspicious that his death wasn't an accident. Such tragedy for a small town, Susan thought. She continued to maintain an interest in Sylvia's case because she'd never forgotten that tragic summer day when Little Bill was brought into the emergency room.

She had to do something this time. She would never forgive herself if she didn't.

After much thought, Susan spoke with authorities and told them what had happened that terrible day back in 1973. Both police and District Attorney Jacobs questioned her.

It was obvious that they, too, thought Little Bill's death was more than an accident. They took Susan very seriously and for that she was extremely grateful.

* * *

CHAPTER THIRTY TWO

For dust thou art, and unto dust thou shall return.
Revelation 6:8

The Kinston Free-Press reported on the Billy White murder daily. Details were sketchy at first, but with each passing day, citizens learned more of the facts behind the crime. As information was revealed, there were also details about two other deaths that occurred in Sylvia's life.

In late February 1992 police reopened the investigation into Sylvia's second husband's death. While reports contended Ipock's death a suicide, this was never confirmed because an autopsy was never performed. There were many family members that swore Leslie didn't commit suicide, said he just wasn't the type. As far as they knew, there was nothing in his behavior to indicate he was depressed or upset about anything that would be considered out of the ordinary.

With this second death coming into the limelight, there was also a third death that was newly regarded as suspicious and that was Sylvia's step son, Little Bill. With newspapers reporting the details of Sylvia's conversations with James Lynwood Taylor, someone in an authoritative position was bound to stand up and take notice.

Detective Bennet Simms of the Lenoir County Sheriff's Department, certainly took notice. Working alongside SBI

Agent Eric Smith and Agent Bill Slaughter, Detective Simms assumed full responsibility for solving the mystery of the child's death.

After weeks of interviewing family, neighbors and friends, Simms and Slaughter both felt sure they had enough evidence to request Little Bill's body be exhumed for an autopsy and further investigation.

Thursday July 16, 1992 was a sad day for the White-Murray families as the final resting place of Little Billy White was desecrated. Their youngest family member had been put to rest all those years ago and now it had come to this. However, Steven, Teresa and Danny all suspected there was more to their little brother's death and were comforted that in the hands of professionals, they might learn what really happened that warm summer day in 1973.

The mechanical sounds of the backhoe as it plunged its steel edges into the hard earth were the only sounds heard at Pinelawn Memorial Park while Bennet Simms and Bill Slaughter waited for Little Bill's casket to resurface. Both men thought it a sad day in their careers as law enforcement officers because both knew the child's death hadn't been an accident. Of course, it was up the medical examiner and a jury to determine this.

After several minutes, chains were attached to the metal that encased the coffin and it was brought to surface. Unbeknownst to all who observed such sadness, there was also a news reporter for Channel 12 who was filming the scenario. Since dawn Paul Dunn had been hiding behind several trees in hopes of catching the macabre sight on film. He was sickened by what he saw. He continued to film the exhumation, but his heart was no longer into the assignment.

Bill Slaughter watched as Pinelawn attendants hoisted

the casket into the back of the medical examiner's van. With a sigh, he and his fellow officers returned to their vehicles. They would follow the van to Chapel Hill, North Carolina where, finally, after almost twenty years, justice was being sought in the tragic death of a toddler.

* * *

CHAPTER THIRTY THREE

Anyone can stop a man's life, but no one his death; a thousand doors open on to it

John D. Butts, M.D., Pathologist for the Office of the Chief Medical Examiner in Chapel Hill, North Carolina had performed hundreds of autopsies. Even so, performing an autopsy on a child was never pleasant, especially when their death was unintentional.

Once the body arrived in Chapel Hill and all the required paperwork was completed, Dr. Butts began his examination. At approximately 12:15 P.M. July 16, 1992 the steel casket bearing the remains of Billy White II was opened. Bennet Simms, Bill Slaughter and M. M. Hatcher remained during Dr. Butts' autopsy.

Dr Butts dictated the following. "The body is received in a sealed steel casket; on opening he is lying on his back clothed in a blue striped jacket over a light colored shirt and blue shorts and underpants. He has a pair of socks on. Pull-up boots are present at the foot of the casket but are not on the feet. The flesh of the body is almost entirely gone with a small residual piece of decomposed tissue lying on the vertebral column. There is a trocar button (*a sharp-pointed surgical instrument)* enclosed in a cannula *(a metal tube used for insertion into the body to draw fluid)* used for withdrawing fluid *(from the abdominal cavity*) lying in the abdominal area."

The evidence of injury. "An occipital (*the curved compound bone forming the back and part of the base of the skull.*) skull fracture is present on the right beginning at the parieto-occipital suture line just to the right of midline and extending inferiorly and slightly medially to the foramen magnum. The fracture is four inches in length. Along the margins of the fracture, both overlapping and undermining is noted under the dissecting microscope. Near the most superior portion of the fracture line, over the superior occipital bone, there is a one-inch by one and a half-inch area of excavation of the external table. Minor fracture lines extend from the mid-portion of the fracture anteriorly and laterally to the parieto-occipital suture line and to the left into the mid-portion of the left half of the occipital bone. The location of these fractures and areas is noted on accompanying diagrams and photographic documentation is made." The medical examiner continued with the external description of the child. "The body is skeletonized and weighs six pounds. His hair is blonde, there are no eyes and his natural teeth are present. His liver is not detectable; rigor is also undetectable." The internal exam of the child revealed, "no significant remnants of the internal organs are noted. Small amounts of both dried and residual soft tissue material is noted along the ribs and vertebral column and within the cranial vault. The bones lie in normal anatomical relationship. They are removed and examined individually for evidence of fresh or old trauma. None is noted.

"The neck region is explored and the three portions of the hyoid are identified and are intact. No remnants of the thyroid cartilage are noted. There are no foreign materials in the neck region. As noted, no recognizable internal organs or internal organ fragments are present.

"No evidence of injury, other than that described in the

skull is noted. The skeletal remains appear to be in a state of maturation consistent with the age of the decedent. Teeth are present in the mouth and show normal development. Ten upper and lower teeth and the second permanent molars are noted embedded within the alveolar ridge. Decalcified sections of skull from the areas of apparent new bone growth on the external table show immature bone spicules above thick lamellar bone consistent with new bone formation beneath periosteum raised by *hemorrhage*."

Dr. Butts' summary and interpretation. "This was a four-year old white male child who was dead on arrival at Lenoir Memorial Hospital on June 21, 1973. The child was brought there, not breathing, with fixed and dilated pupils. There was a history of aspiration of a foreign body, and a plastic garment-type bag was pulled from deep in the throat by a nurse (* By a physician, then given to a nurse.) At the time of the child's death, the medical examiner report indicated that the child had sucked in the bag. Subsequent to this incident, the mother (stepmother) has been charged in the connection with the death of her husband (this child's father), and statements have allegedly been made indicating that his death was not an accident. Since no autopsy was performed on this child at the time of his demise and possible charges in his death are being pursued, it was deemed advisable and in the public interest to have his body exhumed and examined.

"At exhumation, the body shows marked skeletonization with essentially no recognizable soft parts left. The bones lie in normal anatomical location and have the appropriate appearance for his age. No evidence of any fracturing of the skeleton is noted with the exception of the skull, which shows a *recent healing fracture of the right occipital bone. I age this at between one and three weeks prior to his demise.*

There is evidence of subperiosteal bone growth on the surrounding occipital bone, suggesting there was an extensive hematoma in this area. It is unlikely, given the historical circumstances and the evidence of survival, that this fracture is directly related to the child's death. The fracture is extensive enough, however, that it would be surprising if the injury that caused it was not part of the child's history.

The amount of force necessary to produce a fracture of this size could have easily rendered this child unconscious, would undoubtedly have been extremely painful, and the accompanying hemorrhage would have produced a palpable bump on the back of his head. Could this be what Little Bill referred to all those years ago when he told Steven, "I was felled?" It's apparent when Sylvia White failed to kill her step son by pushing him onto the stone fireplace in the house on Hodges Road, her next step was obviously suffocation.

"The cause of death, however, in this child, in my opinion, based on the history, is asphyxiation secondary to a plastic bag being lodged in his throat. From the description of the bag as being wedged deeply into the throat itself, I am of the opinion that this could not have been an accidental event. Accidental asphyxias in children are caused by small objects easily inhaled or swallowed and typically occur in smaller children. *I do not believe a child of this age could intentionally force a plastic bag of the size described that deep into his airway."*

Cause of death: Asphyxiation

* * *

CHAPTER THIRTY FOUR

The price of justice is eternal publicity.

For years prior to the murder of her husband, Sylvia White would never miss an episode of the television program, "America's Most Wanted." When learning this, one can only contemplate, why? Did she have a secret that she thought the popular program might reveal, or did she simply enjoy watching con artists, thieves and murderers such as herself see how long they could actually get away with their crimes? I could hazzard a guess and say it was a bit of both.

On September 28, 1992 Sylvia Ipock-White was formally charged with the murder of her step son. The indictment was returned by the Lenoir County Grand Jury just minutes after two SBI Agents and a Lenoir County Deputy testified. Is this the news that Sylvia hoped would never be aired on her favorite television program?

After she was charged in her step son's death, family members, acquaintances and even her ex-husband crawled out from beneath the cracks. "You see that look in her eyes, you might as well move out of the way because there's hell to pay." Woody Taylor told reporters when he learned his former wife had been charged with the child's murder. "None of this surprises me. I've always felt she had a problem. She's never learned to love."

Again, there was talk. A former secretary whose employer shared office space with Billy White said this in 1973 when she learned that Little Bill died. "As I live and breathe, she killed that child." When she heard Billy White was murdered her first words were, "If they're smart, they'll look at his wife. I'm as sure as the sun will come up tomorrow that she had him killed."

"I never saw much of a relationship there," said a woman who operated the day care Little Bill attended. "I didn't see much of a running up, hugging, picking him up-type situation. His hair was always disheveled and his clothes were dirty."

"It's mighty suspicious for a young'un to choke on plastic," Leslie White, Billy's older brother said. "The little boy was scared of her. Every time he came out here, if he did something, like if he was eating or setting the table and he turned over a glass, or spilled something, he would go crying and hollering, 'Don't tell my mama, don't tell my mama.'"

For the next few months the District Attorney would build his case against Sylvia. The media went crazy. Stories were on the news daily and in the newspapers. After much publicity, Sylvia's attorneys Eugene Jenkins and Bob Whitley, asked for a change of venue.

"Our jury pool is contaminated as a result of adverse publicity. Jurors from another county would be less likely to know the history of the case and the publicity surrounding it." Jenkins said. "It is my opinion, negative publicity is that which tends to expressly state or imply that she is guilty. She should be assumed innocent until all evidence is presented."

Jenkins and Whitley were granted a change of venue. The trial was moved to Williamston, North Carolina, about fifty miles from Kinston. On April 12, 1993 jury selection began and was completed. The citizens of Martin County were ready to perform their civic duty.

A month earlier potential jurors had been selected for Ernest Basden's trial, which had been moved from Jones County to Duplin County at the request of defense attorneys William Craft and Charles Henderson. Three weeks later a Superior Court found Ernest Basden guilty of first degree murder in the death of Billy White, Sr. The jury deliberated a mere one hour and twenty minutes. Later that week Duplin County jurors were asked to decide on the proper penalty for Ernest Basden. After two days of deliberations, the jurors returned with a sentence of death. Ernest Basden had resigned himself to spending the rest of his natural life behind bars. He was not that concerned that he'd received the death penalty because he knew it would take years for the Courts to hear his appeals that would follow his conviction.

* * *

CHAPTER THIRTY FIVE

History is little else than a
picture of human crimes and misfortunes.

April 12, 1993

With a jury of seven women and five men, plus two female alternates, District Attorney Don Jacobs was ready to do what the State of North Carolina paid him to do.

After the jury was empaneled, Don Jacobs proceeded with his opening statement. "Ladies and Gentlemen of the Jury, I want to tell you that we appreciate your cooperation, your attention and your bringing your time and effort and your intelligence to weighing out the facts of this matter and applying the law that the Court will give you to decide this matter.

"Coming out of the Eighth Prosecutorial District, we know that it's somewhat of an imposition for you to come down here and decide cases that come from another area, although you're citizens of North Carolina, we humbly appreciate it. Thank you.

"This case arose, as you have heard, in 1973. Only in 1991, late 1991, early 1992 did the defendant establish, as you will hear, a relationship with a gentleman by the name of Lynwood Taylor. You will hear him testify. We will show you that in the course of that relationship he was solicited to kill Billy White, Sr."

Jenkins objected and was overruled. After the jurors were sent out of the courtroom he asked that the court allow him to have a continuing objection to Mr. Jacob's opening statement. He explained that he did not want to continue to interrupt Mr. Jacobs saying he deserved an opportunity to remain uninterrupted, but for purpose of preserving his record on appeal, Jenkins wanted a continuing objection on record. His motion was noted and granted. The jurors were brought in.

Mr. Jacobs resumed his opening statement. "Ladies and Gentlemen, the State will prove to you that in late 1991, early 1992 Lynwood Taylor was approached by Sylvia White to kill her husband, Billy White, Sr. We will prove to you that Mr. White was an insurance salesman in Kinston, highly respected, fairly prosperous man; that he and Sylvia White had been married a number of years; they had married in the late seventies after Billy White II, was born; that they had both been married previously. His first wife, with the birth of Billy White, II, through complications of pregnancy, had had difficulty and was incapacitated which led to a divorce. Billy White and Sylvia White, living in the same general area, became associates; they dated then wed. Her family moved in with Billy White's family. They had a number of children, each from their previous marriage; they all lived together there in Kinston on Hodges Road. June 21, 1973 approximately at three o'clock in the afternoon, Mrs. White shows up in the emergency room of the Lenoir Hospital, Billy White, II, with her, dead on arrival at the hospital." He gazed at the jurors.

"You will hear and will have explained to you the human anatomy of the throat, the mouth and the way in which humans breathe, aspirate air and inspirate air, also. You will see a chart about how the trachea is in the front of your throat, somewhat protected by what we commonly call the Adam's

Apple, a cartilage that is right here that will protect probably one of the most vital organs of your person." He paused, looked at the defendant and continued. "There is behind the trachea another little cartilage that separates it from the esophagus which runs into your stomach, that food passes down."

District Attorney Jacobs was very precise as he described the parts of the throat. He took several minutes to lay out a diagram for the jurors. After this lengthy narrative, he proceeded to tell the jurors a story. "In 1991 Lynwood Taylor will tell you that in his conversations with Sylvia White, 'I don't want to kill anybody. I can't kill anybody. I'll see if I can't get somebody to kill him,' and you will hear in that conversation the encouragement that will prove to you the encouragement of Taylor for killing, Sylvia White saying, 'Killing another human being is not all that difficult. I had a step son that I killed and it was better off.' We will prove that to you.

"And you will hear the circumstances about the relationship and you will see various medical people who will give you their opinion, that in their opinion it could not be an accidental death. This has been a road map for you to understand where the State's case is going and we will call witnesses to show to you what we contend the killing of Billy White, II amounted to.

"There will also be some evidence for you to sift through wherein we will show you that Billy White was exhumed, dug up from the grave, casket and all, and transported to the medical examiner's office in Chapel Hill for a pathologist, a professional in his field, to determine cause of death, to analyze the remains, and to report to you the findings of that body.

"There will be some evidence that I have not mentioned here that I would suggest to you has some bearing. We invite you to listen and invite you to remember the anatomy that you have heard in the opening statement, that you will hear very quickly after the case begins from a long-time medical examiner."

Jacobs thanks the jurors, then Jenkins was next to give his opening statement.

"Good morning, ladies and gentlemen. I didn't get a chance to introduce myself yesterday. My name is Gene Jenkins. With my partner, Mr. Whitley, we're representing Mrs. White, and it is our objective or our duty in the case to help you examine the evidence in the case and for you to determine at the conclusion of the trial whether you are fully satisfied and entirely convinced that on June 21, 1973, Billy C. White, II did not die as a consequence of an accident. His Honor will tell you that if you don't find that they've proven beyond a reasonable doubt that he did not die as a result of an accident -- "

"I'm going to object," from Don Jacobs.

"-- that you will find her not guilty." Jenkins finished saying.

The Judge interrupted. "Mr. Jenkins, you may not argue and try and persuade these people. You can outline what your evidence is going to show. You may not attempt to persuade the jury to your position."

"Yes sir, Judge. Now, Mr. Jacobs, he told you a number of facts, but there were some things he left out, and I don't want to be redundant but I think it is important to that crucial issue which I just phrased for you, which I just set up for you.

"Now, I think it's important for you to know that June 21, 1973 was a pretty day. This was a period of time you will learn when the children were out of school. Billy C. White, II had a number of brothers and step brothers who were living in the home with him at the time he choked on this piece of plastic.

On that day, these children, ranging in age from seven to twelve, were at the neighborhood swimming pool, which is no more than a block away when this is supposed to have happened; there were neighbors out in the yard, in the houses on the same street. This was a neighborhood, a small community and after Sylvia White realized that this child was choking, she grabbed him up, got in the car and she drove down the street that they lived on, blowing the horn frantically trying to get some help. A neighbor working in the yard near her home plugging centipede grass saw her and came over to her and said, 'Lady, you're in no condition to drive, move over.' He drove her to the emergency room. He will describe for you a mother with a child in her arms catatonically rocking back and forth saying, 'Help me, help me. Please help me.' When they get to the emergency room they rush in with the child and *it's* delivered to the emergency room personnel."

Mr. Jenkins refers to Little Bill as "it," the same as Sylvia did when she told James Lynwood Taylor about his death.

"They take the child behind the doors and the doors close. A number of different people saw the child. They also saw the piece of plastic which Mr. Jacobs has talked about, which I think will take on some importance in this case. They also saw Mrs. White. Those people include Dr. Frank Sabiston. You're going to learn that Dr. Sabiston was a Board Certified surgeon; he was one of several people at that time acting as medical examiner in Kinston. He was the doctor that was called to remove foreign objects from individuals when there was a problem. They relied on Frank Sabiston so to that extent he was an expert in Kinston at that time in this field.

"You're going to learn that the emergency room nurses, two of them, will testify. One nurse came from the operating room and got Dr. Sabiston involved when she asked him to remove the plastic from the child's throat. Like Dr. Sabiston, the nurses knew there were other children in Mrs. White's care. Dr. Sabiston had to take a device while the child was in the emergency room. You will hear this described."

Gene Jenkins continued with his opening statement. He gave jurors an overview of his case. He told them that the actual plastic removed from Little Bill's throat would not be produced. He told them that Dr. Butts' findings were not based on actual physical evidence. He explained how James Lynwood Taylor had given four different statements and in one of them, Lynwood claimed to have been lying when he said Mrs. White killed her step son.

He concluded his opening. "We believe if you listen to the evidence and you listen to it carefully and you pay particular attention to what was done in 1973 that you will return a verdict of not guilty."

* * *

CHAPTER THIRTY SIX

How easily murder is discovered!

After the defense finished with their opening statement, it was time to present the witnesses. First to be called by the state, Peggy Chrisco one of the attending nurses in the emergency room the day Little Bill was pronounced dead.

Peggy testified what her role was in the emergency room that day, told the court she was terrified to have any kind of plastic in her home because this tragedy had left such an impression on her. She explained she remembered it so well because it was her first experience with the death of a child in her nursing career. She remarked how unusual Little Bill's death was. She testified to speaking with law enforcement officials during their investigation of Mr. White's death. She also testified about the discrepancy of which physician was the actual signer of Little Bill's medical chart. The chart indicated that Dr. Brimmer did, but Peggy was sure he was never in the hospital emergency room during the time of the child's death. The date of his signature was in question. Peggy was questioned further by Jacobs, then she was dismissed.

The next witness called was Susan Manning. (Susan's last name was Waters at the time of Little Bill's death.) She was questioned about her educational history, her marital status and if she had children. She was asked if she was one of the attending nurses in the emergency room on June, 21 1973. She explained her role and that she had discarded the piece of plastic that Dr. Sabiston removed from Little Bill's throat into the sink. She also stated that she hadn't seen Dr. Brimmer in the ER that day. Susan was asked to fashion a piece of plastic the same size as the one she remembered being removed from Little Bill's throat. This was passed around for the jury over much objection from Mr. Whitley. After a few more anatomical questions, Susan was allowed to leave the witness stand.

The State called their next witness, Dr. Richard Page Hudson, Jr. Several minutes were spent asking Dr. Hudson about his education and experience. A pathologist, who interned at Johns Hopkins Hospital, also attended the Department of Legal Medicine at the Harvard Medical School where he took a fellowship in forensic pathology. He was also the Chief Medical Examiner for the State of North Carolina for eighteen years. After it was established that Dr. Hudson could be labeled an expert in the field of pathology, specifically, forensic pathology, Jacobs began his questions.

He began by questioning Dr. Hudson on anatomy, particularly, a diagram that was displayed in the courtroom showing the internal portions of the mouth, throat and the respiratory system.

"Dr. Hudson, state whether or not, in your opinion, that the chart more accurately illustrates the esophagus in its collapsed state than it does in its broadened state while it's actively passing something through it."

Dr. Hudson spoke directly to the jury. "It's my belief that this diagram illustrates the open esophagus."

Dr. Hudson resumed explaining the parts of the throat, mouth and respiratory system. He told Jacobs that the size of the trachea in a small child, such as a four-year-old would be smaller than what the actual illustration depicted.

"Now, doctor, assuming the nurses attending to a young four-year-old child in the emergency room, the child we've called dead on arrival, DOA, report that a wad of plastic, of similar size (two inches when wadded up) nature, and consistency, was removed from the child's throat by use of a Kelly Clamp, that visually the plastic could not be seen in the throat even after depressing the tongue, and that only with an instrument of some sort of scope was a doctor able to see it in the throat. Do you have an opinion satisfactory to yourself whether or not such an object could have been swallowed by the child?

"Yes," Dr. Hudson said.

"What is your opinion?' Jacobs asked.

"I don't believe such a structure could be swallowed."

"Can you explain to us what you base your opinion on, Dr. Hudson?"

"Well, even allowing for the elasticity or stretchiness of the pharynx, the back of the throat, this to me is too large a structure to get back there just by the swallowing motion. There is not enough strength in breathing in or in trying to swallow for a child to pull a mass this big down."

Jacobs maintained this line of questioning. "Doctor, in your opinion, could a child take a mass that size and insert it into that area of the throat by himself making it self-inflicted?"

"I would find that extremely unlikely. May I ask in my consideration of this do I consider it with or without the tape?" When the ball of plastic was passed around for the jury to examine, it was held together by a piece of tape.

"Without the tape." Jacobs said.

"Right," said Dr. Hudson.

Jacobs asked, "Have you made those assumptions?"

"Yes. That would make it more difficult to swallow

because the volume, the spread of it, would be larger and greater than it is as a mass like this."

"Assuming that an individual is alive when an object of that nature is inserted into the throat, what are the defensive reactions that the body would involuntarily cause to come about because of the threat to its person?"

"So-called gag reflexes is probably one of the first and most immediate and one of the most, in a sense, violent and predictable. Foreign objects about the throat set up a reflex that generally results in movement of the structures of the throat to reject or expel the object that there, whether it's the end of a spatula or a foreign body, or some other foreign body. That's part of it. The other would be that when something obstructs the airway or makes breathing difficult there is a similar reaction, that is to blow the airway free of whatever it is that's obstructing it."

"Doctor, other than the years that you were the Chief Medical Examiner for the State of North Carolina, did you monitor all of the cases reported to the medical examiner system?" Jacobs asked.

"The office did. I, or one of my associates, reviewed all of the reports that came in question."

"During the years that you were at the Chief Medical Examiner's office and the years after you left, have you ever known of a situation of a material such as a plastic garment bag in that size and that shape having accidentally been aspirated or drawn into the airways of a small child?"

Mr. Jenkins objected and was overruled.

"No," Dr. Hudson answered.

"I assume though, Doctor, in order for you to maintain your teaching credentials you have kept abreast of the literature?"

"I've tried." Dr. Hudson said.

Jacobs assumed his questioning of Dr. Hudson. The courtroom was so quiet you could've heard a pin drop.

"Now, assuming a plastic laundry bag of that size, that consistency was in fact removed from deep in the throat of a four-year-old child by use of a Kelly Clamp and that it was wet, that it was not in shreds, it had not been tattered and there was no evidence of chew or bite marks, on or about it, do you have an opinion satisfactory to yourself, based upon reasonable medical certainty, whether or not that object was forced in the throat by outside force or whether it could have, in fact, been swallowed?"

"Yes." Dr. Hudson said.

Again, Mr. Jenkins objected and was overruled.

"What is your opinion?" Jacobs questioned.

"In my opinion, the material, the plastic was forced into the throat."

Jenkins objected and was overruled by the judge.

"Now, in your parlance, doctor, for the Medical Examiners' purposes, you would have had to designate whether that particular death was of a certain type, would you not, on your report?"

"Yes, sir."

"How would you have characterized the death of that nature?"

Another objection from Jenkins was overruled.

"That type of death would be classified as homicide."

Mr. Jenkins made a move to strike and was denied.

"Define a homicide for me, sir?" Jacobs asked.

"A homicide, as the medical examiners office interprets and as I interpret it is in accordance with the statute, is the death of another . . . the death of a person at the hands of another due to that person's intent or gross neglect."

"Now, Doctor, assuming a four-year-old child, that consistent with your opinion it was indeed forced down the four-year old child's throat, are there any sort of reflexes that the four-year old child would make voluntarily and involuntarily to ward off the threat to its person if that child were indeed conscious at the time it was forced into its throat?"

"Yes. There would be reflexive movements of the hands and arms."

"Tell me about that. What would the child do to protect itself?" Jacobs asked.

"I would expect the child to have its hands and its mouth trying to ward off the foreign object or to remove the foreign object and then there would also be the internal actions of rejection that I have previously referred to."

"Now, Doctor, assuming the child was unconscious or dead at the time the plastic was forced into the throat, would there be any such reflexive actions at that time?"

"If there is unconsciousness, no sir. There could be a little bit of the internal gag reflex with unconsciousness really depending on the degree or depth of the unconsciousness, but I would not expect the hands to be reactive."

"Now, assuming a plastic polyurethane laundry bag, the type of material you've got there, is used as a weapon to suffocate, in your experience how is that a dangerous instrument? Can you explain that to us?"

An objection was made and overruled.

"It's dangerous in at least two ways. One is that it has a clinging characteristic about it so that it's a danger particularly to the smaller children. Infants who even with the motions of their arms may not be able to get it away from the face. The other danger is that if it's in the form of a bag and the bag is over the head, over the body, then the child may not be able to get out of that and again also has the clinging characteristic of the plastic at that point."

Jacobs showed Dr. Hudson what was marked as State's Exhibit Number Four. He asked the doctor to identify it. He described the plastic garment bag. Mr. Jenkins then objected to the bag being given to Dr. Hudson because it was not the actual bag removed from Little Bill's throat. He was overruled.

"Dr. Hudson, how would you use that bag in order to place it over the head and suffocate?"

Another objection from Mr. Jenkins and it was overruled.

"One, that the bag might be pulled over the head and then held about the neck, or pulled down further and held down around the chest, or if there's such an expanse that even without putting the head of the body in the bag, it would be put over the face and the head and held tightly."

"Do you have an opinion of how long it would be before a four-year-old child would be rendered unconscious from having its airway obstructed by external means by use of the bag?"

"Yes to the extent I could offer a range. Asphyxiation situations including the kind you are referring to may cause unconsciousness and even death in a matter of a few seconds or it may take a minute or two. There's that much variation from person to person in the way they react to lack of oxygen."

"And at that point would they be dead or would they be unconscious?"

"More typically I believe a person would be unconscious for a while and then dead, but I'm convinced that in some instances death occurs almost simultaneously with unconsciousness."

"Doctor, assuming that an object the size and shape and consistency as State's Exhibit Number One, was removed from the throat of a four-year old child somewhere in the pharynx area, that upon examination of the body there were no markings of any type on or about the body at any place other than the bandage on the ankle, a very small bandage of gauze nature with tape, no mashings on the neck, no markings on the chest, no bruises, no blows, do you have an opinion satisfactory to yourself that at the time that an object of that nature was being inserted into the throat the child was most probably living, unconscious or dead?"

"I don't, for the reason that it could be any of the three."

Mr. Jacobs thanked Dr. Hudson for his testimony. Mr Jenkins then began his cross examination. The defense was very thorough in their cross. They asked Dr. Hudson about the physical aspects of the throat, those of a small child versus that of an adult. Dr. Hudson said there was a size difference. This went on for a while before Jenkins questioned him about defense wounds, or signs of defense.

Jenkins continued to question him about the medical examiner's office in 1973 when Dr. Hudson was employed by the State. Dr. Hudson recalled the case and was sure that either himself or someone from his office had made an inquiry, then admitted at that time that there was not sufficient cause to warrant further investigation into the child's death.

Jenkins asked Dr. Hudson if he had any hands-on experience with Little Bill's case and he said no. Jenkins stated to Dr. Hudson that his opinion was formed based on things he was told, then asked if the variables of the case could change his opinion. Dr. Hudson said it could. Mr. Jacobs objected and there were no more questions at that time for Dr. Hudson.

Jacobs felt the day in court had gone well. He had made

his point. It was highly probable that Sylvia Ipock White had placed the garment bag over Little Bill's head, suffocating him before she crammed the ball of plastic down his throat.

* * *

CHAPTER THIRTY SEVEN

Into each life some rain must fall,
Some days must be dark and dreary.

The State called their next witness, Anita McGirt. During her direct examination by Mr. Jacobs her professional credentials were established, her marital status and what her duties were as Operating Room Manager at Lenoir Memorial Hospital in 1973. She told the DA she knew Billy White and that she also was acquainted with Anita, Billy White's first wife. She also claimed to know Sylvia Ipock White as well.

Mr. Jacobs asked her if she remembered anything about that summer day in June, 1973.

"I was working in the operating room that day, the seven to three shift." Anita said.

"At the end of your shift, what did you do?" Jacobs questioned.

"We had surgery late and I came down to go home and I was going out through the emergency room."

She paused and Jacobs shot another question. "When you went out through the emergency room did anything attract your attention?"

"Yes. Billy and Sylvia were leaving through the emergency room door and I stopped and asked somebody what had happened, why they were there."

"Do you see the Sylvia that you referred to here in the

courtroom that you saw leaving from the hospital at that time?"

"Yes, sir."

"Where is she?" Jacobs inquired

"Sitting beside Mr. Jenkins."

"Now, after you discussed with the two nurses what may have happened, did you go and see anyone?"

"Yes."

"Who?"

"Little Billy."

"What was Sylvia's demeanor like when you spoke to her before you went in to see Little Billy?"

"I didn't speak to her. She and Billy were leaving and she was very upset."

"Where was Little Billy in the emergency room?" Jacobs asked.

""He was in the main emergency room lying on the table."

"What did he look like?"

"A dead little boy. I mean, just lifeless."

"Do you recall his color?"

"A little blue, but not like it was a long time or anything."

"Pardon me?" asked Jacobs.

"He was a little blue, but not like it had been a long time."

"Do you recall where the bluishness was?"

"Around his lips. It meant oxygen deprivation. When you don't have enough oxygen going into your lungs to oxygenate your blood it becomes more saturated with CO 2 and it makes it more blue in color." Anita said.

"Did you go over and examine Little Billy?"

"Yes, sir."

"Do you recall who all was in the emergency room at that time?"

"When I went in the emergency room there was nobody there except him. The nurses, or the one that had been comforting Sylvia. He (Little Bill) was by himself and I just walked in."

"Do you remember what nurses you saw in the emergency room at that time, or later, while you were there?" Jacobs quizzed.

"The only one I remember was Susan."

"Now, did you examine Little Billy to see if you could determine what might be wrong with him?"

"The nurses outside had told me what had happened and I just went in held his hand, standing there with him."

"So did you observe anything taking place with Little Billy?"

"Dr. Sabiston came in. He said something about what had happened. I said he had swallowed some plastic and I asked him if he would please take it out."

"After you told him that, did Dr. Sabiston do anything toward removing the plastic from the throat?"

"Yes sir."

"What did he do?"

"I asked him would he please take the plastic out. I knew the child was dead, but I just wanted him to take the plastic out of his throat, so he did."

"Were you there when Dr. Sabiston extracted the object?"

"Yes, sir."

"Did you see the object?"

"Yes, sir."

"Tell me in your words what it was." Jacobs stated.

"It was a piece of plastic that was wadded up. When he took it out, it unfolded."

"After it was extracted from the throat, how quickly did it unfold?"

"Immediately."

"Do you know what condition it was in?"

"It was in one piece. Nothing fell apart. It was wet on the outside. I didn't touch the plastic, but it looked damp on the outside."

"Did you see any markings on or about it? Any ragged edges? Was it one-ply or two- ply?"

"I didn't notice any markings, or ragged edges. It seemed to be one-ply."

A few restless watchers adjusted themselves in their seats. The questions were becoming monotonous, but Jacobs knew he had to be thorough in his questioning.

"Can you tell me the size, shape and contour it appeared to be when you first saw it come out of the mouth?"

"It was about a handful. It just kind of opened up like a flower would open up in your hand." Anita said.

"Can you give me any idea of the diameter of the flower, the measurements of the flower?"

"It was a big handful." Anita replied.

"Do you have an opinion satisfactory to yourself whether or not you personally could have swallowed that much plastic?"

Mr. Whitley objected and was overruled.

"I don't think I could have." Anita said to Mr. Jacobs.

Mr. Jacobs continued his direct examination. He asked Anita if she remembered seeing Susan and Peggy in the emergency room that day. She did, but did not recall seeing Dr. Brimmer when he asked her about him being there at the time of Little Bill's death. Mr. Jacobs asked Anita about Dr. Sabiston's reputation in the medical community. She agreed it was very well respected. The DA had no further questions and Mr. Jenkins approached the witness for his cross examination.

He asked her if she was aware of the publicity surrounding Mr. White's death. She was. He asked her when she first spoke with investigators about Little Bill's death. She told him it was in the spring of 1993. He then went on to ask her if she felt there was anything she observed in the emergency room in 1973 that made her suspicious about Little Bill's death. She remembered that all of the nurses in the ER that day made comments on the size of the plastic because it was so large. The court took a brief recess and the next witness was called.

* * *

CHAPTER THIRTY EIGHT

The golden guess
Is morning-star to the full round
of truth.

Don Jacobs called Dr. Frederick Payne Dale to the witness stand. He went through his usual list of questions when a new witness was called; education, occupation, where they lived and if they were retired or continued to work. Dr. Dale said he practiced for thirty years as a general surgeon at the Kinston Clinic.

"Did you know Billy White, Sr.?" Jacobs questioned.

"Yes sir. For approximately twenty-five years."

Dr. Dale testified that he knew Billy White Sr. because he had purchased insurance from him. Later Billy's eldest son Danny became good friends with Dr. Dale's son. He said Danny had spent many nights in his home as a youngster. Because of this acquaintance Little Bill was seen by Dr. Dale two weeks prior to his death for a burn he sustained on his left ankle. Dr. Dale testified he was not sure who brought him to the office on June 15, 1973 and again on June 19, 1973, but would assume it was Billy White Sr., since he had signed an insurance form.

"In what capacity did you see Little Bill as a patient?" Jacobs asked.

"I saw in him relationship to an incompletely healed burn of the left ankle."

"Where was Little Bill examined?"

"In our office at the Kinston Clinic."

"How severe were the burns?" Jacobs inquired.

"At the time they appeared rather superficial for a second-degree burn."

Jacobs asked him to define what a second-degree burn was. Dr. Dale explained it was a burn that involves the epithelium, the outer skin.

"Did you make notes about your treatment and what you observed?"

"At the first visit they appeared as I mentioned in my notes, they were rather superficial as far as second-degree burns, although it had been two-and-a half-weeks. On the return visit one area had completely healed and the other was clean."

"Was it your opinion that on the 15th of June, 1973 that the burns had been inflicted as early as two-and-a-half-weeks previous?"

Jenkins objected and was overruled.

"I had no reason to doubt the statement that it had occurred two and-a-half-weeks prior."

"Does that appear in your medical records?"

"Yes, sir."

"Doctor, what treatment did you prescribe for Little Bill?"

"I gave him a treatment for Phisohex soap, which is a mild antiseptic soap and continued saline washes and an ointment which removes the debride."

"Did you bandage the wound?" Jacobs asked.

"Very lightly, if we did. I don't have any recollection."

"What type of bandages would be required for a wound of this nature?"

"Very little."

"Now, Doctor, did you see any burns up and down the leg that would necessitate a bandage from the ankle up the leg?"

"No, sir."

"Would you have prescribed as a treatment bandages covered with plastic up the entire leg?"

"No, sir."

"Plastic over a burn, what would that do for the healing process of a burn?"

Dr. Dale answered, "It would increase the likelihood of infection and increase the moisture and debride that would result from the heat that creates heat, plus it restricts the limited amount of oxygen that would get to it."

"State whether or not in your medical opinion to apply a plastic bandage or plastic covering to a burn wound would be contrary to good, acceptable medical practice and procedure?"

"Yes, sir it would. It definitely would."

"Now, when Little Billy was in your office, you observed the size of his neck, his throat, his general size as a young boy?"

"Yes, sir."

"If you would have observed any abnormality on or about him, state whether or not you would have noted that in your chart?"

"Yes, I would assume I would. Yes, sir."

"Now, I show you an exhibit used for illustrative purposes only, Doctor –"

"Objection!" From Jenkins.

Overruled by the judge.

Mr. Jacobs proceeded. "This has been marked State's Exhibit Number One." He showed him the wadded up piece of plastic. "Doctor, based upon your expertise as a medical practitioner, whether or not you have an opinion satisfactory to yourself an object of that size, that consistency, of that quality, and excluding the tape which is there just to hold its shape, could this accidentally be swallowed by Billy White in your opinion?"

An objection by the defense was overruled.

"In my opinion it would be difficult as this is presented to me. It would require a lot of extenuating circumstances for it to happen. That's the only thing I can say."

Mr. Jacobs passed the witness to the defense.

Mr. Jenkins approached the witness stand. "Dr. Dale, are you saying that it could happen? Is that right sir?"

"In my opinion it would be difficult to understand how it could happen, but I'm not saying it absolutely could not."

"If that piece of plastic is smaller, it becomes more possible that it could have been swallowed b the four-year-old child that you saw in 1973. Isn't that right, sir?" Jenkins asked.

"The relativity of the thickness would be important." Dr. Dale responded.

"Would it be fair to say that as the object gets smaller the possibility of it being swallowed becomes more likely or more possible?"

"The thinner it is, I would say so. Yes."

A different line of questioning began.

"You practice medicine with Dr. Sabiston, don't you?"

"Yes, sir."

"Can you state whether he had a specialty in removing foreign objects from the throat and/or airways of people who might have been presented at the emergency room at or about that time?"

"He did have expertise in that area."

"Can you tell the jury a little bit about that expertise?"

"Dr. Sabiston had training in esophagostomy and

gastronomy in Florida where he trained. He would have knowledge of the pharynx, larynx, this region."

"Was there an ear, nose and throat specialist practicing in Kinston in 1973?"

"I can't recall the exact year his brother, Walter came to practice in Kinston."

"Up until Walter came Frank Sabiston, he was the person that was to be called if there was some need for an examination into the esophagus or that sort of thing. Is that right?" Jenkins questioned.

"If he was on call, he would have been. It would be up to the emergency room physician to call, you know, whichever one he wanted to."

"When you saw the child in your office with the burns on his left ankle can you state who brought the child to your office?"

"I have inferred here that his father signed the insurance records and so I assume he brought him." Dr. Dale stated for the second time in his testimony.

"Now, the two burns that you saw, was there anything about them that would cause you to form an opinion that they were intentionally inflicted?" Jenkins asked.

"No sir. I didn't entertain that I did at the time."

"And if there had been something suspicious about those burns, don't you believe that you would have noted that and written them down on your medical records."

"Suspicious?"

"In terms of whether they were intentionally caused or whether they were . . . . "

" – If I had had some reason you put it down. Yeah."

"Can you read your medical records to the jury Dr. Dale? Will you read the entry for June 15, 1973?"

"It says, 'Two areas unhealed but appear rather superficial. Will continue to soak and return on Monday.'"

"I'm going to stop you there. You say, 'continue to soak.' Does that mean that the ankle was being soaked at that time?"

"Apparently it was."

"Will you continue to read the entry for June 19?"

"You want me to finish this?"

Jenkins nodded. "Yes, sir. I'm sorry, I thought that was the entry."

"Was 'given Phisohex soap and to continue to use Elay (sic).'"

"What is Elay?"

"It's an ointment that's a debridement."

"And so 'continue' again implies that someone had prescribed Elay (sic) for that burn?"

"I would assume that, yes."

"Okay. Is that the end of your entry for June 15?"

"Yeah."

"Would you read the entry for June 19?"

"'One area of ankle completely healed,' and then the other just has a period there and it says, 'but still is fairly clean,' so I assume I'm talking about the other was still fairly clean."

Jenkins continued with this line of questioning. He wanted jurors to know someone had cared for Little Bill's wound enough to clean it and when it wasn't healing properly, they had taken the time to see that he had proper medical treatment. Jacobs, on the other hand wanted jurors to question this burn. If it had been inflicted two to two-and-one half weeks prior to Little Bill being taken to Dr. Dale's office, had it been more serious? Possibly a third-degree burn? It was hard to guess what the jurors were thinking.

CHAPTER THIRTY NINE

The good die first,
And they whose hearts are dry as summer dust
Burn to the socket.

The next witness called was Robert Johnson, Regional Vice President for McNeal, which owns Pinelawn Memorial Park. He confirmed that Billy White Sr. was buried there as well as Little Bill. He explained on that June 25, 1992 he received a court order to exhume remains of Little Bill. He confirmed that the funeral home van took the casket to Chapel Hill and said the remains were out of his supervision for approximately one day.

Imelda Pate, Assistant District Attorney for Lenoir County began questions for the next witness, Manley Michael Hatcher, who was with the Identification Department. He explained what his duties were; going to crime scenes, collecting evidence, storing evidence and recording evidence. He told Ms. Pate that he was at Pinelawn Cemetery the day Little Bill's remains were exhumed. He told her Detective Simms and Agent Slaughter and Agent Smith were also at the grave site. He was there when the casket was removed, and said he was present when Agent Hunnicutt took photographs of the coffin before and after it was opened. He validated that the casket had not been out of sight at any time since its interment. Mr. Whitley was asked if he wanted to question the witness and he declined.

The next witness called was Charles Leslie White, Mr. White's brother. He was questioned by Don Jacobs. He went through the usual round of questions. Age, address, employment.

Jacobs asked, "After Little Billy was born, how soon after that was it that you had contact with Little Billy?"

"Me and my wife kept him for about five, six, seven months. I don't remember how long. After Billy and his first wife separated we kept him until he was old enough to go to Kiddy College."

Leslie White talked about Little Bill. He said he was a very good child. He and his wife Bonnie wanted to adopt him after Billy White Sr. separated, but Billy wanted to keep his family together. He said he never observed anything wrong with Little Bill during the time he and Bonnie cared for him. He explained the White family dynamics as best as he could to the District Attorney, then told about the sad day of Little Bill's funeral. He said he had loved Little Billy and almost went crazy when he learned of his death. He said Sylvia said he'd choked on some plastic, but he hadn't heard anymore details at that time because they were all shocked and grieving. Questions were brief from the defense, then Leslie White left the witness stand.

On the morning of April 14, 1993 court reconvened. After several motions were heard, and a few housekeeping matters attended to, Don Jacobs called his star witness, James Lynwood Taylor to the stand.

Mr. Taylor testified how he met Sylvia Ipock White. He was then questioned in minute detail about their interactions during the planning of Billy White's death. Numerous objections came from both sides. He told the court he was promised nothing in return for his testimony.

Defense attorneys were adamant about getting Mr.

Taylor's testimony about his involvement with Billy White's death thrown out. The DA explained to the judge. "There is absolutely no way we can explain to the jury how she could have trusted him and how she would make what the law calls 'a declaration against her own penal interests' or an admission or a confession under the circumstances to this man (James Lynwood Taylor) unless we show the circumstances and their relationship. It's all bound together and it was an inducement to a conspiracy and the conspiracy was formed at that time. It is a part and parcel of her confession to James Lynwood Taylor."

After hours of legal maneuvers were made from the State and the defense, Jacobs was allowed to resume questioning James Lynwood Taylor.

After dozens of questions, James Lynwood Taylor is questioned by Mr. Jacobs. He asked James Lynwood Taylor what he told Sylvia about taking a life. He told him he had told Sylvia there was, "No way I can take a mans's life. There's just no way I can do it."

"What did she tell you when you told her that?"

"She said, 'It's not that hard to do. I had a step child. I put a bag over it until it stopped breathing. It was better off.'"

* * *

CHAPTER FORTY

Our body is a watch, intended to go for a given time. The watchmaker cannot open it, and must work at random. For once that he relieves or assists by his crooked instruments, he injures it ten times, and at last destroys it.

Don Jacobs called Dr. John Butts as his next witness. His professional credentials were verified. He told the jury he had testified over three hundred times in his role as Chief Medical Examiner for the State of North Carolina. When questioned if he had any experience investigating deaths by suffocation in young children he replied that he had indeed. The anatomical areas of the throat and its abilities were discussed at great length. He told Don Jacobs he had viewed the original death certificate and that he felt there was reason to file a supplemental death certificate.

"Did you in the supplemental death certificate report your opinion based upon reasonable medical certainty and under your investigation and your findings as to the probable instrument of death and how it occurred?" Jacobs asked.

Jenkins objected and was overruled.

"I concluded that this child, Billy White II had died as a result of obstruction of his air passages by a foreign body, in this particular case a plastic bag, and that being of the opinion that he could not have unintentionally swallowed it; it indicated it had been forced down his throat." Dr. Butts responded.

"Did you in examining the bones of Billy White II, did you notice anything of medical significance to you?" Jacobs asked.

Jenkins objected again. He was overruled.

"The most significant finding was of a healing fracture of the skull."

"Can you tell me how serious an injury like that was to the child?"

"It was a serious injury. Not so serious that it caused his death, but serious enough that I stated in my opinion it should have caused a great deal of pain. A child would also have had a big knot on the back of his head, a hemorrhage or a bruise on the back of his head. I would have expected it would have been evident in his past medical history that he suffered some type of serious fall or blow to the back of the head that others around him would have noticed."

"State whether or not in your opinion a fracture of that type is consistent with being struck in the back of the head with some blunt object, with considerable force?"

Jenkins objected, and as was becoming the norm, he was overruled.

"That factor could have incurred in such a fashion." Dr. Butts said.

It was now time for Mr. Jenkins to question Dr. Butts. He asked him why Little Bill's death wasn't fully investigated in 1973. Dr. Butts said that each investigation was investigated; however, he admitted that some deaths were not investigated in 1973 as fully as they are today. Dr. Butts told the court he had spoken to Dr. Sabiston about his findings. Then Jacobs objected.

This is where one can only wonder why Dr. Sabiston wasn't called as a witness. At the time of Little Bill's death, he had only been practicing medicine a few years. Was he truly that unknowledgeable about a field he claimed to be an expert in, that he could go up against his colleagues in the medical profession? Or when Little Bill's body was exhumed and autopsied almost twenty years later. Was he afraid that he had made a mistake? Did he fear legal action? I can only say that when I spoke with Dr. Frank Sabiston while researching this book that he was very blasé. It was my opinion that he could have cared less about this entire incident and that he couldn't see what all the fuss was about. I was never privy to the DA's reasons for not calling him as a witness, and the defense would not speak with me. So, again, one has to draw their own conclusions.

* * *

CHAPTER FORTY ONE

Women love the lie that saves their pride, but never an unflattering truth.

Ernest Basden was the next witness called by the prosecution. Jacobs immediately made it clear to the jury that Ernest Basden was charged with first degree murder in the death of Billy White. He also told the jurors that Ernest Basden's conviction was on appeal. He asked him if he made the decision to testify on his own. Ernest said that he had. Jacobs asked him if he had been promised anything in return for his testimony. He said that he had not.

"When you were with James Lynwood Taylor riding around, did he say anything to you about what Mrs. White had told him?" Jacobs asked.

Ernest nodded. "Lynwood said that Mrs. White had killed her step son. She had put a plastic bag over its head."

Mr. Whitley objected and was overruled.

The rest of Ernest Basden's testimony was about his arrest and conviction. He told the jury that he had received the death penalty for killing Mr. White.

Pat Mewborn was next to be called by the state.

"How long have you known Sylvia White?" Jacobs quizzed.

"Since May of 1991."

Pat explained that she had known Mrs. White before

when they had both worked at the mall. Her husband moved into to Billy White's office to share space. She said she worked for her husband when he shared an office with Billy White.

She and her husband became friends with Sylvia and Billy. They would eat out together and sometimes after work Billy would invite them over for a cook out. She said that she had seen Sylvia the day after Billy White Sr. died. She told the court that she sometimes saw Sylvia as many as two or three times a day after Billy White Sr. died. She took her places. To the cleaners, to the bank and to a psychiatrist. And to the beauty shop.

"Did you ever see an individual at Mrs. White's home after her husband's murder by the name of James Lynwood Taylor?"

"Yes. One day I had gone to her house to take her to see the psychiatrist and he came up underneath the carport with another fellow. She talked to him and she talked to somebody about the house. I guess it was about three or four days before Mr. White died. She asked him to come in and they went into the kitchen. I was in the den."

More objections from the defense that were overruled.

"The first time you saw James Lynwood Taylor come to Sylvia's home, how long was it before Billy White's death?" Jacobs asked.

"I would say two-and-a-half weeks."

"Did Sylvia White ever introduce you to Lynwood Taylor?"

"No, sir."

"Was there ever any explanation given for him being there?"

"The first time that he came she was in the back getting dressed because I was going to take her to the psychiatrist. I told her there was this man there and he looked rather bummy looking and she said she couldn't imagine who that would be and she went to the kitchen door, and talked to him underneath the carport."

"How long did she talk to him at that time?"

"It was probably about five minutes because I was on my way to take her to see a psychiatrist."

"Anybody else there?"

"No, sir."

"Did you ever have the occasion to talk with Sylvia White about Little Billy White, II?"

"Yes, sir."

"Tell me when that occurred, the best you can remember."

"She was keeping Tony's little girl and I had stopped by."

"Can you give me a time reference?" Jacob asked.

"This was just before Billy was killed in January."

"Tell me what she says and what's going on."

"Well, I pulled up in the driveway and she had her little granddaughter and she's a real pretty little girl. I commented how much she reminded me of my older daughter. She told me she had to watch her like a hawk and I asked her why. She said, 'Well, she just gets into everything.' She commented that since the other little boy had died and I asked her what she meant by "the other little boy" because I didn't know that they had had a son and she told me he had died."

"Did she tell you how he died?"

Another objection from Mr. Jenkins that was overruled.

"She said the plastic bag that was on the garment bags were like some the cleaners used. He liked to pull it off and pretend like it was chewing gum. I said, 'Wasn't he sort of old to be doing that particular type of thing?' She said they always had to get on him and always had to spank him for doing that. She said this particular morning that the kids had all gone to school and that he was at the kitchen table eating a bowl of cereal and she had just gotten on to him prior to that because he had some of this in his mouth and she made him spit it out. She said when she went back to get dressed and when she came into the kitchen he was laying on the kitchen table with his head on the table. She said that she just knew that he probably had some of that wrap in his mouth and she tried to get it out and so she picked him up in her arms and she was driving down Hodges Road and she saw a guy on the side of the street and she stopped and he helped her. He went to the emergency room with her."

"Did she tell you how she tried to get it out?"

"She said she stuck her finger down his throat."

"Did she say anything else to you about that occasion?"

"No, sir."

"Did she ever mention anything about Little Bill being burned?"

"Yes."

"Tell me when it was that you had a conversation about him being burned?"

"Somebody had told me that he had been burned and the one day that I went up to her home and I asked how . . . somebody told me he had been burned."

"Now, when you go up there to the house, how does it come up about the burns on Little Billy?"

"We just got to talking about kids and I told her that I had heard that he was burned and I asked her what had happened."

"Objection. Overruled."

"You can answer."

"She said that he used to always like to go help Billy with the charcoal grill. I asked her what did she mean. She said that he wanted to help his daddy and he went out and put the charcoal on the grill and he struck the matches and he got on fire. I asked her what did she mean. She said the day before that Billy had been mowing the yard. He had set the gas tank down to fill up the lawn mower and that some of the gas had spilled there on the grass and by the next day it had ignited and I told her, I said, 'Sylvia if he mowed the yard that night and this was the next afternoon, I can't believe that the grass would catch on fire.' She said it did and that was all that was said."

Whitley made a motion to strike and was denied.

After she was questioned by the defense she was allowed to leave the courtroom.

The DA and defense attorneys attended to more housekeeping matters. One in particular; did Sylvia White have any property that could be sold in order to pay a public defender. A witness for the prosecution did not show up and that hurried things along, though made no difference in the outcome of Sylvia White's trial. This witness was simply going to testify about the warning label on a garment bag. Since it had already been established, the DA explained to the jury what had happened to his last witness.

The State rested their case at that point.

Mr. Jenkins asked the judge to hear a couple of motions outside the jury's presence. They were asked to step into the jury room. Once they were out of the courtroom, Mr. Jenkins proceeded.

"Your honor if it please the court, we'd be moving pursuant to 15A-1227 to dismiss for insufficiency of the evidence."

The judge responded, "Denied."

"Judge, at this time before we make a decision or a statement about presenting evidence, could we have about five minutes to confer with Mrs. White, please?"

"Yes, sir."

Sylvia and her attorney left the courtroom and returned a few minutes later.

Mr Whitley, "Your honor, at this time in view of the prior rulings on motions, we elect to rest."

Members of the jury had been waiting to see if Sylvia White would defend herself. Apparently, her attorneys felt she didn't stand much of a chance.

Next on the agenda was the charge to the jury.

* * *

CHAPTER FORTY TWO

For twelve honest men have decided the cause, who are judges alike of the facts and the laws.

The Honorable William Griffin, Jr. addressed the members of the jury. "You have heard the evidence in this case. The next order of business is for the attorneys to have a chance to speak to you to try to persuade you to adopt their view of this matter. Before that is done I am required by law to have a conference with the attorneys out of your presence about the instructions that I'll give you and this will take a while. I suspect the best course of action would be to let you all go this morning and ask you to come back at one o'clock so that we will have these matters out of the way."

Judge Griffin asked Mr. Jacobs if he had any requests for instructions. He said that he did not, but the principal charge was first-degree murder; second-degree murder and involuntary manslaughter or not guilty.

Mr. Jenkins was asked if he had any special requests for instruction to the jury. He did and gave the judge a copy of this request. Jenkins asked for first degree-murder, second-degree murder and not guilty. There were special circumstances for the manslaughter charge. Those were neglect supported by testimony of the witnesses who had testified that they had heard Sylvia talk about Little Bill chewing plastic, saying if she knew he was doing this, then it was gross negligence as far as the law read pertaining to manslaughter. Jenkins asked the court not to boot strap negligence on the incident pertaining to the plastic.

While the jury was still out of the courtroom, the judge spoke to those that gathered in his courtroom who were there observing the trial. They included family and friends of both Sylvia and Billy White.

"It is clear that some of you may disagree with what one side or the other may say in their attempt to get the jury to adopt their view of the case and I don't think it would be appropriate and I will not permit anybody grimacing or disagreeing or shaking heads or anything of that kind. If you feel like you're going to be required to conduct yourself in that fashion, I'll ask you to leave now. All right, are we ready to go forward?"

"Yes, sir," from Mr. Jacobs.

The jury was brought back into the courtroom.

It was agreed with the judge that the defense would start with their closing statement.

"In this case, as I told you in the beginning, the government must prove in order to justify
a guilty verdict on the verdict form, which will ultimately be handed to you, and it's really another way of saying this in order for you to render any verdict other than a verdict of not guilty you must be fully satisfied and entirely convinced to a moral certainty that Billy C. White II did not die as a result of an accident on June 21, 1973. The State of North Carolina or the prosecutor, it is their burden to fully satisfy you and to entirely convince you to a moral certainty that it was not an accident and this is an instruction, I understand, that the judge is going to read to you. That is the law in the State of North Carolina."

Jenkins went over the evidence presented by the State. The medical evidence, the so-called confession he said Mrs. White made to entice James Lynwood Taylor to kill, and the monetary evidence, referring to the insurance policy on Little Bill that Sylvia was co-beneficiary of. He talked about Dr. Butts' and Dr. Hudson's testimony. He spoke of the dimensions of the plastic and reminded jurors that the actual plastic removed from Little Billy's throat was not in evidence. He then spoke about the lack of action when Little Bill died. Three nurses and not one made a single phone call. Nothing was mentioned about Dr. Sabiston's lack of action at the time of the child's death. James Lynwood Taylor's credibility came into question. He told jurors it was very suspect.

He closed his statement with these words. "Ladies and gentlemen, in some ways it's a little like a tapestry. There are bits and pieces of evidence that is almost tantamount to a thread. You have to find those threads. You have to pull them out of the evidence and let it sort of lead along as a detective and put them together, and if you try to make a piece of whole cloth that shows a murder it's got this big hole in it. It deals with that medical evidence or the absence of injury, the absence of Frank Sabiston saying then that he made a mistake, and I believe that it is all consistent with Taylor making the statement and starting the investigation and just the whole negative thing running from there. Thank you."

* * *

CHAPTER FORTY THREE

A child is mourned.

Imelda Pate began her closing argument with a bang. "I hope you remember James Lynwood Taylor testifying yesterday. I hope you remember his statement to Mr. Whitley when he was being cross-examined. 'She got to me. That sweet little old lady with all these problems. She just wouldn't leave me alone. The things she told me that went on in her life. How could that have happened. I just don't understand it. This sweet little old lady who I talked to over a year about how, when and where to kill her husband.'"

"What were her problems?

"The State would contend to that in 1973 she had a problem with a four-year-old step child. A step child who approximately two weeks before he was brought into the emergency room, dead on arrival, is burned, and we never really know how he's burned, because she gives different explanations for the burns to people she tells it to over a period of time. She tells her neighbor, Mrs. Paderick one thing; she tell her good friend Mrs. Mewborn a different story about how that four-year-old child was burned in 1973.

"If a child, whether he be yours by blood or yours by marriage, had been living in the home with you for years, a two to three year period of time and he died, number one; would you not remember the circumstances of his death; and number two, would you not remember the circumstances of him being burned two weeks before that death?

"What does Dr. Butts tell you about what happened to that child approximately two to three weeks before he died? Something that the passage of time could not erase. He tells you two to three weeks before that child died he sustained a blow to the back of his head that caused a skull fracture and it was a blow that one would have noticed. It was an injury that individuals around him would have noticed the difference in the child, but when is the last recorded time that the child was taken to the physician before he died? He's taken to the physician two weeks after the burn, the skull fracture occurring two to three weeks prior to the death.

"Again you've got a small child in your care and custody. Whether he's your own or whether he's your step child, or whether he's just a child in your care, and that child is burned. What would you do the day it happens? Would you not, if it was a serious burn take him to the doctor that day, or would you wait for it to almost heal and take him two weeks later? Well, if you're going to do that, what are you waiting for? Are you waiting for something else to heal other than the wound to his ankle? Something else that a doctor might detect upon examining the child that might make the doctor a little suspicious, and the first time that child was taken to the doctor two weeks after the injury you don't even take him, you're the one that's there when it happened. You're the one that can explain to the doctor how he was burned. What was the burn from? Gasoline? Was it a cigarette burn or was it a burn from a stove? Was a burn from a hot pot? Wouldn't it be important if you were the one who was there to be the one to go to the doctor with that child, to tell the doctor how the child was burned so he could get adequate treatment? But who goes to the doctor with

Little Billy? Who goes to see Dr. Payne Dale with the child? It's not Sylvia. It's the child's daddy. Why would the daddy wait until the wound had almost healed to take his son to the doctor?

"In considering whether or not you want to believe the testimony of James Lynwood Taylor and believe whether or not this woman sitting over here that you have been looking at this whole week would tell him that she killed a child, you have to consider why would an individual confess murder to somebody else?

"Well, you'd do it if you trusted them, wouldn't you? Yeah, you would. And let's talk about that trust that existed between Sylvia and Lynwood.

"They had been talking together for over a year before Sylvia ever confessed to Lynwood about killing this child, and for over a year they had been talking about the construction of the new home. For over a year they had been talking about him putting windows in a new home. No. What had the two of those individuals been talking about for over a year in private? At secluded places where they couldn't be overheard? What had they been discussing? They had been discussing her need to get rid of her husband. 'I'm desperate.' She knew before she confessed to Lynwood about killing that child that for over a year Lynwood could have done what to her? Turned her in to the police; could have turned her in to her husband; could have notified people in the family that she's trying to kill Billy White, Sr. Does Lynwood do that? No. Does a trust factor exist? Has a relationship been formed between those two individuals so that the Sunday before the death of her husband she would feel confident in recruiting Lynwood to find somebody to shoot her husband or to kill her husband and she would feel confident in recruiting that individual to tell him what? When Lynwood tells her, 'I can't do it. I can't kill another man,' she says, 'It's easy.

Don't worry about it. I've done it. I had a step child. I put a bag over its head until it stopped breathing. It was better off.' What a thing to say about a four-year-old.

"How in the world would Lynwood Taylor be possessed of the knowledge at that time concerning the medical realities of the death of Little Billy back in 1973?

"Do you think Lynwood went around and called Peggy Chrisco and Susan Manning and Anita McGirt and Dr. Sabiston and Dr. Butts and Page Hudson and asked them?

"Did this child suffocate in 1973? Tell me. No, he didn't do that, but Lynwood knew how that child died. Lynwood knew that Sylvia confessed to him that she put a bag over the child's head until it stopped breathing and so what did the medical experts, Dr. Butts and Dr. Hudson, tell you about how that child died? Well, they tell you that the piece of plastic found in the child's throat could not have been swallowed and the plastic could only have been forced down the throat.

"Dr. Butts and Dr. Hudson tell you that one reason that they testified to that is because the body, whether you be an adult or a child, your body would not be possessed of the strength and the muscles in the throat to swallow such an object. In chewing such an object to try and swallow it, it would be so much in your mouth to do what? Dr. Butts said you would gag; you would expel it. He termed it as such a foreign object would be expelled from the body by a gag response ir reflex.

"How many of you have ever been to the dentist and they x-ray or clean your teeth or they're doing something and they've got their fingers in your mouth and maybe you've got those little x-rays on the side of your mouth, what is the dental hygienist telling you to do? Breathe deeply and relax so you won't gag. I know you feel like you've got to do it but try to relax so you won't gag and what I (hygienist) put in your mouth won't come out. It's a natural reflex, one we cannot stop. It's like the blinking of your eyes and it's a reflex to protect us. It's a reflex to protect us from choking and dying.

"Why would this piece of plastic be found down Little Billy's throat at the emergency room in June of 1973? Let's explore that.

"For whatever reason we know Sylvia is at home alone with Little Billy. We know on that date that Little Billy about two weeks before then received a blow to the back of the head and his skull had been cracked, and Little Billy, at the same time, is recuperating from a burn. A four-year-old child. Not the best circumstances under which to baby-sit a child in the afternoon in June of 1973. For whatever reason, Sylvia takes a plastic bag, maybe she's mad, maybe she's tired of listening to the child complain. I don't know, but she does as she told Lynwood she did and puts it over his head and she holds it there until he stops breathing. Now, what are you going to do? I've got to explain it somehow. The child has died. He's dead, we can't bring him back. He ain't breathing. What am I going to do? Well, I got this plastic right here in my hand. Wait a minute. Let me see. Let me think. A couple of weeks ago I told Barbara Paderick about the child chewing plastic and I told her out of the clear blue sky after the child's legs had been wrapped up to his hip on the way to Dr. Dale. Dr. Dale never saw plastic on that child's leg. Wasn't it on the second visit when they carried him back for the follow-up visit to check the wound on his ankle, said it was a small bandage on the ankle. Think about that. Isn't it ironic that Sylvia goes out of her way to stop Barbara, her neighbor, that drops in all the time, to show her. Look at Little Billy, his legs are all wrapped up in plastic, all up to here. Sure can't avoid seeing that and look at this in my hand. Look at what he's done. He's all the time got this in his mouth. Is Sylvia not setting up at that point in time how to get rid of that child that was annoying her?

"What does Dr. Dale tell you about putting plastic on a burn? Contrary to all types of medical science, you just don't do it. Barbara Paderick tells you that she sees the child's legs wrapped in plastic up to his hips. She remembers her children telling her the child's arms were wrapped in plastic. My, God, what were they doing to the boy?

"She killed that little boy and she told Lynwood Taylor that she killed that little boy. Lynwood told you, 'If she had left me alone I wouldn't be here now; my uncle wouldn't be on death row. I tried to get Mrs. White to get professional help. Tell them, Mrs. White. Every time we met I said you need professional help, lady.'

"I believe she did. This sweet little old lady with all these problems and poor Billy White, II because in 1973 a medical doctor thought so much of him in examining him after he had died that the only thing he did was after being asked to do so by an operating room nurse, he stuck a Kelly Clamp down that boy's throat, took out the plastic, handed it to Susan Manning to throw away and he leaves. That, members of the jury, is the extent of your investigation into this death in June of 1973 and when Mr. Jenkins stands up and reads off this death certificate that Dr. Sabiston signed stating that he had investigated it, had examined the child, had looked into the surrounding circumstances and deemed it to be accidental, well, I tell you what, I hope that's not the way Dr. Sabiston treats everybody for a medical problem when they go to see him. The only people who investigated this death at the time it occurred were Peggy Chrisco, Susan Manning and Anita McGirt, because they are the only three people that at least took a look at the little boy to find out what he looked like, and what he was wearing. They took the time to examine the plastic, because what do they say that Dr. Sabiston did with it? He never even touched it. He went down the child's throat, grabbed the plastic in the Kelly Clamp, took it out, deposited in into the hand of Susan Manning, her outreached hand, from the Kelly Clamp, he let it go in Susan's hand and she took it and dropped it in the hopper where they put trash at the time that happened to be the sink and this is the only thing this man did to investigate this death. That was what your medical examiner in Lenoir County did to investigate the little boy's death back in 1973 and he never thought another thing about it, until what? Until he began to think that he had to sign this official piece of paper because he didn't sign it until two months later. Yet what do the people who investigate this death tell you about it? I've never seen anything like it before or since. The three people in that examining room in the emergency room who did a medical investigation at the time, who took the time to examine the plastic, who took the time to look at the little boy. 'I've never seen anything like it before or since.' That's what each one of them said in their testimony repeatedly, and they tell you that's how they can remember it so vividly. The only thing Dr. Sabiston is going to be able to tell you is what's on this sheet of paper because that's all he did. He removed it, got rid of it and left because he was off duty, he was through operating for the day. That's how much that doctor cared about the death of this little boy, but when Dr. Butts begins his investigation last year in 1992, and there's an exhumation of the body, what happens? Ha! Dr. Sabiston calls Dr. Butts and Dr. Butts talks to him. I wonder why? And Dr. Butts performs what we would call a medical examination of a death. He talks to the people who were there. He listens to the statements of the nurses, Mrs. Chrisco, Mrs. Manning and Mrs. McGirt. He does an autopsy on the deteriorated body of Billy White, II, finally a complete medical investigation into the death of this little boy, what occurred? A supplemental report of cause of death is filed with the State of North Carolina. That's what occurred, and the supplemental report of the cause of death says that the manner of death is not natural, it's not accidental, it's not suicide. It's a homicide. It's a homicide, members of the jury. It is a planned killing by someone who wanted to get rid of a step child that was in the way. It was a planned killing by this sweet little old lady with all of her problems.

"You tell me. If somebody at the time had cared about Billy White II, when he was at the emergency room who had the power and authority to cause an investigation, if somebody had cared about his death at that time and asked for an investigation, what would they have determined?

"Well, number one, there would have been an autopsy. That would have been one thing that was required by law. I don't know if you would have found anything more or less than what we found. We don't know, but we do know in 1973 for sure you would have found what was on the back of the child's skull. A healing skull fracture. If a medical investigation had been requested in 1973 you would have also had the testimony and statements of Mrs. Manning, Mrs. Chrisco and Mrs. McGirt. You would have also had the financial information of the parties involved, because Mr. Jenkins said to you, that does go toward motive. You know, why do people get rid of other people? Do you do it because you're mad at them in a fit of anger, or do you do it because you might have something to gain from it, or do you do it for a combination of all of this? Well, we know for a fact that for four years after the death of Little Billy White, II, ironically the same period of time that he lived on this earth, for four years this sweet little old lady over here collected insurance premiums from the death of that small child. Was it a reward for looking after the child for the length of time that he lived here on earth? I don't know, but we know she got that money in periodic installments from the insurance company and we know that to be a fact. Well, she didn't know she was going to get it when Billy died.

"I believe most of you told me that you were married. Most of you know what type of insurance policies your spouses are paying on, what's coming out of the household account. Well, Billy, my husband, we're paying on an insurance policy for my step child, but his natural mother is the beneficiary, not I. His natural mother has been committed to an institution, who can no longer care for the child. I'm the one looking after him all the time. I'm the one having to put up with him. Shouldn't I be the one who benefits if he dies? About the same day the daddy takes the child to the doctor so daddy also does what to the insurance policy? The daddy changes the beneficiary to the stepmother. A motive to now begin thinking about talking to Barbara Paderick about the plastic, the plastic that at that period of time there were warnings on the bags saying, what? 'Keep out of reach of small children. This is not a toy.'"

After this lengthy beginning the judge gave members of the jury a ten minute break. A few minutes later they returned to the courtroom where Don Jacobs took over. He spoke about the laws and how things have changed over time. He spoke of all the choices they would have when it was time to deliberate. Guilty of first degree-murder; second-degree, involuntary manslaughter and not guilty.

He spoke about the medical investigation that never was in 1973. He told how Dr. Brimmer tried to file the medical certificate saying "accident." He explained that Dr. Sabiston had filed the death certificate three months after the fact. He told the jury that Dr. Sabiston had already violated the rules and regulations of the Department of Vital Statistics because he was fifty-five days late in trying to avoid that responsibility. He explained how negligent Dr. Sabiston was when Little Bill died.

"Now when does Dr. Sabiston come in to the emergency room? Sylvia White and her husband had already left. We know that because Anita McGirt said when she came down out of the operating room she saw the family. She knew Billy. She went on and saw Little Bill and took him by the hand. Dr. Sabiston came rushing from his office according to a summons because he was the medical examiner. Why couldn't Dr. Brimmer have done it? Because they were suspicious and they told you that they reported in up the channel of command in 1973. The defense will have you believe that there is no suspicion on behalf of the nurses, but they call a medical examiner. They don't call a doctor that can come and certify death on any death in this state, except when it's accidental or homicide, Dr. Sabiston as the medical examiner comes. Sabiston comes in and we're analyzing him now. We're analyzing his opinion on this death certificate. He gets down there, gets the plastic out gives it to Susan and leaves. Won't even sign as the attending physician. You know it and I know it and he knew it was required because he is a doctor, he's a surgeon. He didn't know the other nurses in the room, but he knew Anita. Won't even do the paper work. Careless? Reckless? Whatever you want to call it.

"Dr. Butts said he x-rayed the remains and found skull fracture. Did Dr. Sabiston take the time to put in the orders and say, 'Take the kid to the x-ray room and see if there is anything that I can't see with my eyes about the kid.' Didn't do that. Didn't care. I looked at the kid. I listened to the mother and she makes a self-serving declaration. Good family. Right side of town. I'm busy. I'm a surgeon, I've got to make money. This ain't much money, if any at all. Nurse, enter in the record that I want the kid taken down to x-ray. I want the kid's x-ray's to see if anything else is wrong with him. Reasonable precautions. Not done. Leaves. Won't do his paperwork. He has denied by his callousness, by his insensitivity, by his brazen actions, an autopsy, an x-ray, a further investigation medically of what was wrong with the kid. What if there had been plastic in the kid's stomach? In his lungs? He's denied that.

"What else do we know about Dr. Sabiston? When he begins to be under examination, when his opinion is under examination, he becomes defensive because he calls Dr. Butts. Wouldn't you liked to have a phone tap on that telephone line between Dr. Butts and Dr. Sabiston? Wouldn't you like to have heard what Dr. Sabiston told Dr. Butts, the Chief Medical Examiner for the State of North Carolina? Dr. Butts apparently didn't think much of it because he rejected it."

Imelda Pate finished her part of the closing argument.

One can wonder, if Dr. Sabiston had been more thorough in his investigation of Little Bill's death, in all probability, Billy White Sr. would be alive today. And if Dr. Jilcot had ordered tests on Billy White when he went to the doctor complaining of stomach troubles, he might have suspected that his patient was being poisoned.

I made several visits myself to Dr. Jilcot's office in hopes of acquiring Mr. White's medical records. I had permission from the family, I even contacted the attorney, P.C. Barwick, who represented Mr. White's estate. I was told by Dr. Jilcot's wife that I would have to check with the North Carolina Board of Physicians. Mrs. Jilcot said she spoke with the North Carolina Board of Physicians and they advised her not to release Billy White's medical records. When I contacted them, I spoke with David Henderson, Attorney for the Board of Physicians. He stated he had no record of any telephone conversation pertaining to this matter. Why? I have no idea. I only know that it was very suspicious when I had legal permission to do so. Why did Dr. Jilcot's wife and staff refuse to allow me access to Billy White's medical records? Could it be they were afraid of a lawsuit? If he had ordered the proper testing for his patient, maybe Dr. Jilcot could've warned Billy that someone was poisoning him. Again, he might be alive today. Two doctors. Two deaths.

* * *

CHAPTER FORTY FOUR

The beginning of the end.

April 16, 1993

The trial lasted a week. Jurors were ready to go back to their lives and the attorney's had appeals to file and legal matters to deal with.

Judge Griffin gave his instructions to the jury. He explained reasonable doubt to the jurors. "Reasonable doubt is a doubt based on reason and common sense, arising out of some or all of the evidence that had been presented. Proof beyond a reasonable doubt is proof which fully satisfies or entirely convinces you of the defendant's guilt."

He then asked the jurors, "Are any of you sick, infirmed, unable to go forward at this time? All of you are healthy and able to continue in the matter?" They all nodded in an affirmative response. The judge released them to the jury room and asked them not to deliberate the case until they received the verdict sheet.

The jurors received the verdict sheet and began their deliberations at 9:31 A.M. One hour and forty-four minutes later, they knocked on the door indicating that they had reached a verdict.

"Let me say this while the jury is coming in. I don't want any expression by the group assembled here, one way or another, no matter what the verdict is going to be." Judge Griffin said.

"Mr. Smith," Judge Griffin asked, "You're holding the verdict sheet. Does that mean you're the foreperson?"

"Yes, your Honor."

"Has the jury reached a unanimous verdict?"

"We have Your Honor."

"Mr. Smith, if you will hand the verdict sheet, please, to Mr. Brickhouse and let him hand it up here to me. You can relax there."

The Bailiff handed the verdict to the judge.

"Mr. Smith, you have returned as the jury's unanimous verdict that the defendant was guilty as charged. Is that the verdict of the jury, Mr. Smith?"

"That's true," Mr. Smith stated.

"So say all the jurors?" the judge asked.

He received an affirmative response from all the jurors.

"Is this anything further before I dismiss the jury?"

"Judge, we'd ask that you poll the jury." Jenkins said.

The jury was polled and all responded in the affirmative that they had reached a guilty verdict.

The judge asked the prosecution and the defense if either had anything to say in regard to sentencing. They did not.

"Mrs. White, if you will stand up please." Judge Griffin said.

She stood up and faced the Judge.

"The judgment of the Court is, Mrs. White that you be imprisoned in the Department of Corrections in quarters provided for women for the remainder of your natural life."

After her sentence, Sylvia White turned around and looked at her family. Tony, Todd and her sister Marianna, "Don't cry, it'll be alright."

CHAPTER FORTY FIVE

All's well that ends well.

After court the White family members congratulated Don Jacobs, Imelda Pate, Eric Smith, Bill Slaughter, Bennett Simms, Sheriff Ayers and Sheriff Billy Smith.

Bill Slaughter reached out to give Teresa White-Murray a hug. He had tears in his eyes. "Watch yourself," he warned.

Bill Slaughter and Eric Smith assured family members that Sylvia would be watched for suicide attempts. After spending several minutes with those who fought for justice for Little Bill, family members went downstairs to watch as Sylvia was led from the courthouse to the Women's Correctional Center in Raleigh, but she was already gone, or so they thought. The family gave statements to three local network television stations. Imelda Pate and Don Jacobs gave statements to the press. Right after the Don Jacobs finished his statement, there was a big clap of thunder. Danny White yelled, "It's a sign from God!"

A few minutes passed and a police officer from Williamston and a large plain-clothed officer came running outside where the crowd was starting to break up. Family members heard through the crowd that an Emergency Medical Unit had been called, but no one would tell them anymore more than that.

A few minutes later, an ambulance backed up to the

door of the Sheriff's Department. They carried Sylvia White out on a stretcher, with oxygen, yet no one would tell family members what had happened.

The family loaded up in their cars and followed the ambulance to the Emergency Room. Police cars were all over the parking lot and wouldn't allow anyone near the doors to the Emergency Room. White family members waited outside for forty-five minutes.

An older male bailiff came outside and spoke with the family. He told them what had happened. Apparently Sylvia White had locked herself inside the bathroom. Police officers had to break the door down to get her to come out. When they found her inside, she had tried to swallow a plastic laundry bag with several unidentified white pills wrapped up in the plastic.

About that time, Sheriff Ayers arrived and told the family he would get them more details as soon as he learned of them himself. About twenty minutes later he came outside and told members of the press and news media that his instructions for securing Mrs. White had not been followed.

"We had to kick the door in," Ayers told reporters. "She was never unconscious. I took her around the neck so she couldn't swallow and Deputy Ward took it out of her mouth."

Later it was learned that Sylvia had been seen passing an envelope and a legal pad to a friend who was in the courtroom. Apparently, she had asked a bailiff if she could pass a note to her family. She gave three envelopes to her friend and told her to give them to Tony, Todd and Marianna. Maybe the pills had somehow been passed back and forth during this transaction?

Without assistance, Sylvia White left the hospital. She was asked by a reporter whether the suicide attempt proved her guilt. "No, this just proves I wasn't guilty." She said. This time she was placed in shackles as she was led to the police vehicle that would take her to Raleigh. When she got inside the car, family members clapped loudly. Teresa White-Murray waved at her stepmother and said, "Goodbye." She grinned and thought good riddance.

* * *

EPILOGUE

November 22, 1993

Though it had been more than a year-and-a half since Billy White's death, there was still the matter of Sylvia's participation in the murder-for-hire scheme and James Lynwood Taylor's role in the murderous plotting. Even though Sylvia had already been convicted in April 1993 for the 1973 death of her step son, Little Bill, she had yet to be tried for her husband's death. Ernest Basden had been tried in March 1993. He spent eleven years on death row.

In Clinton, North Carolina District Attorney Bill Andrews was preparing to present testimony on November 22, 1993 when out of the blue James Lynwood Taylor pleaded guilty to murder in the death of Billy C. White shortly before his trial was to begin the next day. His attorney's Louis Foy and Rivers Johnson told this to Judge Henry Stevens before the trial began. They said he had not made a plea bargain with the State.

Taylor told Judge Stevens he had made the decision to plead guilty after much discussion with his wife, mother and his attorneys. Bill Andrews knew nothing about this until that Monday morning. The jurors chosen to hear Taylor's trial still had to hear the States and the defenses' cases as they presented their evidence.

Taylor agreed to testify against Sylvia White, postponing his sentencing until after the trial for her role in her husband's death.

District Attorney Bill Andrews told reporters, "Lynwood has agreed to testify against Sylvia, I think now that he has pleaded guilty and admitted his guilt that he will make a more efficient witness."

Defense attorneys would use this delay to prepare for Taylor's sentencing hearing.

In January 1995 the North Carolina Supreme Court heard arguments aimed at winning a new trial for Sylvia White, stating she was convicted of Little Bill's death because much of the evidence that was used against her should never have been presented to the jury. Daniel Pollit of the Durham Appellate Defender's Office had hoped to direct the Justice's questions toward the testimony of two key witnesses for the State when he defended his brief on Mrs. White's behalf.

September 1995, four years and two days after Billy White's death, Sylvia was preparing to stand trial in Sampson County Superior Court because of pre-trial publicity, as ruled by Judge Henry Stevens. Both the state and the defense approved of this location.

When asked about her stepmother's upcoming trial, Teresa White-Murray said, "I want her to have a fair trial, and I want them to do whatever it takes for her to get a fair trial."

In November 1995 the Supreme Court refused Sylvia White's request to review her murder conviction. A January 1996 date had been planned for her trial in her husband's death.

In order to avoid the possibility of execution, Thursday December 7, 1995 Sylvia Ipock White pled guilty to second-degree murder and conspiracy to commit murder. A friend said, "She's not guilty of this! She had to plead guilty in order to save her life."This hearing was fast and uneventful when Judge Henry Stevens accepted Sylvia White's plea, then sentenced her to a second life sentence, plus an additional ten years for the conspiracy charge. She is serving the sentences consecutively. She will be ninety-years old before she is eligible for parole.

In February 1996, in a Wayne County Courthouse in Goldsboro, North Carolina, jury selection began for James Lynwood Taylor's sentencing hearing. Once the jury began their deliberations after a two-day period in March 1996, totaling seven hours, jurors sentenced Taylor to life in prison.

Almost eleven years after the murder and fighting for his life to the end, claiming he deserved clemency, Ernest Wesley Basden was put to death Friday, December 6, 2003 at Central Prison in Raleigh, North Carolina.

James Lynwood Taylor remains incarcerated at Pamilco Correctional Facility in Bayboro, North Carolina. He is serving a life sentence. He will be up for parole in 2013.

Sylvia Ipock White remains in custody in Raleigh, North Carolina at Central Prison. She is serving two life sentences, plus ten years for conspiracy. She will be ninety-years-old before she in eligible for parole.

It had taken over four years to bring this unlikely trio to justice. Lives of those involved would never be the same. Teresa White Murray and her two brothers had lost their biological mother to mental illness, only to be followed by the death of their youngest brother, then they lost their father and last, their stepmother, the woman who perpetrated the chain of events that caused the family so much loss.

Teresa White Murray and her husband Johnnie have continued on with their lives. They have raised a happy child and continue to reside in North Carolina.

Steven White had a few years that were troublesome. He resorted to the use of drugs, but having the same inborn strength as his sister, Teresa, he rose above that and is now happily married and raising a family of his own in South Carolina.

Danny White struggled with the loss of his younger brother and father and still struggles daily to overcome the abuse he suffered by his stepmother. He is a family man and raises his children with love and patience. He resides in South Carolina.

Jeff Ipock, Sylvia's oldest son by her first marriage to Woody Taylor, lives in Raleigh, North Carolina. After a tragic accidental fall from a balcony, he spent many months in a coma. Now his days are filled with learning to live his life as he did before the fall. He has good days and bad days.

Tony and Todd Ipock did not participate in any interviews pertaining to this writing.

Leslie Ipock's family continue to live in Kinston, North Carolina. They know their brother did not commit suicide and can only hope that Sylvia will confess to his death in the future.

In 2000 when I first started researching this book, I tried to visit Sylvia, Lynwood and Ernest in prison. Ernest Basden was willing, but Sylvia still refused to admit that she had done anything wrong and could not understand my interest. James Lynwood Taylor was very polite when he refused an interview. However, I was able to correspond with each of them through letters.

I wrote a letter to Ernest Basden's attorney, Matthew Martin. In the letter I listed several questions that I wanted Ernest Basden to answer. These are the questions as asked and answered, via email from myself to Mr. Martin. Mr. Martin advised Ernest Basden not to answer some of my questions, stating, "It's not that he's being uncooperative, his lawyers are just being prudent." The question Ernest Basden was advised not to answer, "Tell me your feelings when you shot Billy

White then walked away?" Mr. Martin suggested I refer to the trial transcript regarding the events on the night of Billy White's murder. The following is a duplicate of our correspondence.

SB – What is your legal name and marital status?
EB – Ernest West Basden, November 18, 1952. I'm divorced, have one step child and another step child was murdered in Kinston a few weeks ago by her husband.
SB – What is your education?
EB – I am a high school graduate and I served in the U.S. Army where I received an honorable discharge.
SB – Tell me about your childhood in as much detail as possible.
EB – I am the youngest of ten children. My dad was sixty-four when I was born. My dad had a farm, but we were poor. When I was fourteen, my mom was killed in a car crash. This was devastating to me. When mom died, it was like losing both parents at the same time, because it crushed my father to lose my mom.
SB – Were you close to James Lynwood Taylor growing up?
EB – I spent a lot of time as little boys with my nephew, Lynwood (who was older than me) when we were growing up because we were close to the same age.
SB – Did you trust him? (James Lynwood Taylor)
EB – I trusted Lynwood.
SB – Had you ever heard of Billy C. White prior to his death? Leslie Ipock?
EB – I did not know Billy White, Sylvia White or Leslie Ipock before this incident.
SB – When did James Lynwood Taylor first tell you Mrs. White wanted to murder her husband?
Mr. Basden did not answer this question.

SB – What was your reaction?

Mr. Basden did not answer this question.

SB – How long was it before James Lynwood Taylor mentioned Mrs. White wanted to murder her husband before the crime actually took place?

Mr. Basden did not answer this question.

SB – When did you decide to participate in this crime?

Mr. Basden did not answer this question.

SB – Did James Lynwood Taylor or Sylvia White promise you anything?

Mr. Basden did not answer this question.

SB – Did you tell anyone other than James Lynwood Taylor about this event?

Mr. Basden did not answer this question.

SB – Tell me in your own words the story that you told to the Kinston Police when you turned yourself in.

Mr. Basden did not answer this question.

SB – Why did you turn yourself in?

EB – Lynwood's family pressured me to go to the Kinston PD.

SB – What is your relationship with James Lynwood Taylor today? Your family's relationship?

EB – This has torn the family apart. I have no relationship with Lynwood today.

SB – Did Sylvia White ever approach you while you were incarcerated in Jones County? Did James Lynwood Taylor ever approach you while you were incarcerated in Jones County?

EB – I have never talked to Sylvia White. I was incarcerated with Lynwood in the Jones County jail. Lynwood's dad saw to it that we were in the same cell. Lynwood told me that we had to stick together. Once I sobered up, I began to distance myself from him.

SB – How were you treated while imprisoned while in Jones

County?

EB – I was treated okay while in Jones County by the Sheriff. I had some medical problems, so I went to Raleigh for safekeeping. I certainly didn't get the treatment Lynwood got, though, but no one else did either.

SB – Do you feel that you have been given a just sentence for the crime you have been convicted of? If not, explain why.

EB – I do not feel that my sentence was just because my trial was not a fair one.

SB – Do you realize the enormity in taking a man's life?

EB – I do realize the enormity of taking a person's life. I have admitted my involvement with Lynwood in this and sincerely regret it. It is wrong for an individual to take a life and it os wrong for the State to do so.

James Lynwood Taylor's letter.

June 2, 2001
Dear Ms. Barr,

I hope this finds you feeling well and doing good.

I have been disregarding your requests to talk with me concerning the terrible crime in which I was a part of. I apologize for this but it disturbs me that people continue to profit from Mr. White's death. Why are you writing a book? Have you interviewed Sylvia White, Ernest Basden, Tony Ipock Rose and Denny Clark or any of Mr. White's children?

I belong in prison. I had rather be where I am today than go back to the kind of life I was living ten years ago. I only regret deeply that Mr. White was murdered. His murder was a cowardice act for which I expect to spend the rest of my life in prison. I am sorry.

I do not have an attorney. There is nothing a lawyer could do for me now anyway.

I am working to repay Jones County $35,000.00 in attorney fees. I also pay Department of Corrections a per diem each month and a percentage of my income goes to the Victim Compensation Fund. It gives me a good feeling inside to be able to do this. A sense of purpose, and a kind of independence, if you will.

I wish you all the best in your endeavors, Ms. Barr.
With Great Respect,
J. Lynwood Taylor
Philippians 4:11-13

And Sylvia Ipock-White's letter.

Dear Mrs. Barr:

When I received the 1st letter, for which I was not allowed to read, I thought, who could this be, but maybe Suzanne Coulston who was in jail at the time I was, Maybe she had married and was now living in Fla. She was a precious young girl, and I was interested in hearing from her.

First, let me explain, I do not want the money $10 you sent. I have no way of sending that back to you, we are not allowed to send cash through the mails, neither do I have access to a bank or have a checking account. I would ask that you call here and ask that that $10 be taken from my account and returned to you. Feel free to check on the DOC policies for receiving postage through the mails, also us sending cash out in our letters.

My question to you would be, what interest is my life or the lives of mine and Billy's to you, other than monetary gain for yourself?

Billy and I raised six wonderful children, we have precious grandchildren, all whom I love dearly. Billy's mother is in her 80's now, don't you think she has suffered enough heartache. There are many things if she knew concerning Billy could hurt her deeply. He was a wonderful man, but like all humans he had his weakness. Our children have suffered enough, they neither have me or their daddy there for them. Our grandchildren have suffered and will the rest of their lives, so have so many other family members and friends of ours. You say "in all fairness to my family," you would like to talk to me. These people I have mentioned are my family. Since I am the one convicted and I have neither the truth or the facts concerning Billy's death, I can not see any amount of interviewing others can give you these truths or facts. If you do find such a person or persons, please contact me with their names. I have been waiting since the early morning of January 21, 1992 for these answers.

In as you say, "all fairness to my family" I am asking you to consider the heartache and pain this book would cause them for the remainder of their lifetime, for the little monetary gain you would receive. As for me, I can not be hurt anymore, my heart was torn from my chest on January 20, 1992. I do not care about me, only the people both Billy and I loved deeply. Please do not do this to him. God's blessings to you and your family this holiday season.

Sincerely,
Sylvia White

* * *

Readers may email Suzanne at SuzyBarr@aol.com

To order additional copies from the publisher send a check or money order in the amount of 12.95 plus 4.50 S&H to:

The Write Stuff, Inc.
P.O. Box 150205
Cape Coral, Florida 33915

Online orders: SuzanneBarr.com

Visit her web site at www.SuzanneBarr.com

Other books by Suzanne

Mountain Magic

Every Woman Has A Story, "A Mother's Farewell"

And coming in hardcover August 2005
from the Five Star Mystery Line

SIGHT UNSEEN